INSPIRE / PLAN / DISCOVER / EXPERIENCE

ITALIAN RIVIERA

DK EYEWITNESS

ITALIAN
RIVIERA

CONTENTS

DISCOVER 6

EXPERIENCE GENOA 50

EXPERIENCE THE ITALIAN RIVIERA 102

NEED TO KNOW 172

Left: The names of Cinque Terre villages
adorning fish souvenirs
Previous page: The charming harbour of Portofino
Front cover: Dusk falling over Vernazza, Cinque Terre

DISCOVER

View from the Church of St. Peter in Portovenere

WELCOME TO THE ITALIAN RIVIERA

Sandy beaches for miles. Pastel-coloured houses fringing tiny harbours. Chic cities stacked up cliffs and mountains dotted with medieval villages. Known as the Italian Riviera, Liguria is a bewitching region. Whatever your dream trip includes, this DK Eyewitness travel guide is the perfect companion.

1 Hiking the steep coastline near Camogli.

2 Tranquil cloisters at Sant'Andrea in Genoa.

3 The winding alleyways of Cervo.

4 Colourful houses lining Portofino's harbour.

A crescent of land squeezed between mountain and sea, Liguria is Italy's slimmest region, and one of its most dramatic. Life is lived between the beach and the peaks, with fashionable coastal towns overlooked by remote hillside settlements. There are two clearly defined sides to the region, tethered by understated capital, Genoa. The Riviera di Levante (the eastern riviera) is a wild land of rocky headlands and pretty fishing villages; the Riviera di Ponente, unfurling west of Genoa to the French border, is tamer, its resort towns still redolent of their belle époque heyday.

But there's more to the Italian Riviera than its fabled coastline. This is a land rich in history: in Balzi Rossi stand prehistoric caves, while in Luni there are Roman ruins, and timewarp medieval villages dot the mountains. That's not forgetting the churches cantilevered above the shorelines, and the *caruggi* (alleys) of Genoa, which wind through Europe's largest intact medieval centre. With its thriving art scene and innovative food festivals, the region is an alluring mix of the ancient and contemporary.

With so much to see and those beaches beckoning, it can be hard to know where to start. We've broken the region down into easily navigable chapters, with detailed itineraries, expert local knowledge and comprehensive maps to plan the perfect trip. However long you plan to stay, this DK Eyewitness travel guide will ensure that you see the best of this spectacular corner of Italy. Enjoy the book, and enjoy the Italian Riviera.

REASONS TO LOVE
THE ITALIAN RIVIERA

With its rolling hills and undulating coastline, its culturally rich history and its modern status as a chic holiday destination, the Italian Riviera is loved by all who visit. Here are just a few reasons why you'll love it, too.

1 COASTAL VIEWS
Liguria's vertiginous coastline is best seen from the water. Boat trips show it at its most dramatic, and double as ferry routes around the Cinque Terre *(p112)* and the Portofino peninsula *(p108)*.

PICTURESQUE VILLAGES 2
From the multicoloured houses of Camogli *(p122)* to the streets of Portovenere *(p128)* and teeny Boccadasse *(p100)*, Liguria's fishing villages are picture perfect.

3 MEDIEVAL TREASURES
Genoa's Centro Storico is a maze of alleyways that make up Europe's largest intact medieval centre *(p56)*. Explore them to uncover churches, palaces and superb galleries.

GREAT PARKS 4

Natural parks make up about 12 per cent of Liguria, from the coastlines of Cinque Terre *(p115)* and Portofino *(p108)*, to the Antola, Aveto *(p124)* and Beigua *(p158)* regional parks.

LAND OF ART 5

The Roman ruins at Luni *(p130)*, the galleries of Genoa and castles-turned-museums dotting the cliffs: Liguria has centuries of mesmerizing art and culture on display.

HOLY LANDS 6

Romanesque and Gothic churches dot the landscape. Sant'Andrea di Borzone *(p125)* perches in the hills, while Portovenere's San Pietro *(p128)* hangs over the sea.

CINQUE TERRE HIKES 7

Italy's most visited national park, the Cinque Terre *(p115)* is crisscrossed with 120 km (75 miles) of trails. Hike along the clifftops, through vineyards, past churches and into valleys.

PREHISTORIC WONDERS 8

Liguria's cliffs and crags were home to prehistoric people. Today, you can walk in their footsteps in caves at Toirano *(p152)* and find out more at the museum at Balzi Rossi *(p169)*.

9 BEACH BITES

What tastes better than fish scooped straight from the sea? All along the coast you'll find mouthwatering seafood, from platters of fish to the Cinque Terre's anchovies.

FESTIVAL CHEER 10

Italy lives for its festivals, and Liguria is no different. From the Sanremo Music Festival *(p33)* to Camogli's Sagra del Pesce *(p28)*, the calendar is always packed.

A GLASS APART 11

Liguria produces exceptional white wines, including the vermentino of the Colli di Luni area and the intensely minerally, sea-salted Cinque Terre DOC wine.

GO GREEN 12

The Riviera's 19th-century heyday as a holiday destination left a legacy of gardens. Admire the Giardino Esotico Pallanca *(p166)* or explore the Hanbury Botanical Gardens *(p156)*.

Map of the Italian Riviera showing locations including:

Carmagnola, San Damiano d'Asti, Asti, Felizzano, Alessandria, Racconigi, Nizza Monferrato, Savigliano, Bra, PIEDMONT, Alba, Bubbio, Acqui Terme, Fossano, Ovada, Dogliani, Rossiglione, Centallo, Monesiglio, Sassello, Palo, Cuneo, Cairo Montenotte, Dego, LIGURIA, Borgo San Dalmazzo, Millesimo, San Giovanni, Arenzano, Bagnasco, Bormida, Varazze, Limone Piemonte, Vado Ligure, Savona, Garessio, Bardineto, Spotorno, Tende, RIVIERA DI PONENTE *p134*, Finale Ligure, FRANCE, Monesi, Rezzo, Borghetto Santo Spirito, Saorge, Triora, Leca, Albenga, Chiusavecchia, Alassio, Pigna, Laiguéglia, Bajardo, Marina di Andora, Dolceacqua, Imperia, Cervo, Taggia, Ventimiglia, Porto Maurizio, Sanremo

EXPLORE
THE ITALIAN RIVIERA

This guide divides the Italian Riviera, or Liguria, into three colour-coded sightseeing areas, as shown on the map above. Find out more about each area on the following pages.

LOMBARDY

Rivanazzano

Tortona

Novi
Ligure

San Sebastiano
Curone

Rivergaro

Fiorenzuola
d'Arda

Castell'Arquato

Bobbio

Marsaglia

EMILIA-
ROMAGNA

Béttola

Pellegrino
Parmense

Arquata
Scrivia

Ronco Scrivia

Busalla

Vobbia

Ottone

Bedonia

Berceto

Pontedecimo

Casella

Montoggio

Montebruno

GENOA
p50

Torriglia

Farfanosa

Borgo Val
di Taro

Montelungo

Pegli

Doria

Uscio

Cicagna

Borzonasca

Pontremoli

Voltri

Genoa

Nervi

Camogli

Rapallo

Varese Ligure

RIVIERA DI
LEVANTE
p104

TUSCANY

Golfo di
Genova

Lavagna

Sestri Levante

Moneglia

Sesta
Godano

Aulla

Riviera
di
Levante

Levanto

Monterosso al
Mare

Vernazza

La Spezia

Riomaggiore

Lerici

Campiglia

Portovenere

Montemarcello

Ligurian
Sea

0 kilometres 20

0 miles 20

N

GETTING TO KNOW
THE ITALIAN RIVIERA

Spanning around 350 km (220 miles) of verdant coast with the capital of Genoa at the centre, Liguria, or the Italian Riviera, is a delightfully wild strip of land in northern Italy. We've split the region into the Riviera di Levante, to the east of Genoa, and the Riviera di Ponente, to the west.

GENOA

PAGE 50

Liguria's understated capital has a host of remarkable galleries and museums, along with a buzzing port and Europe's largest medieval centre. Despite its charms, you'll find fewer tourists thronging the streets than in other major Italian cities. Historically the capital of one of the world's most powerful maritime republics, Genoa exudes wealth: grand palazzi border the Via Garibaldi, while the illustrious Teatro Carlo Felice has hosted the very best in world opera. Throw in the city's incredible food scene – this is the home of pesto, after all – and Genoa is one of Italy's unsung gems.

Best for
Grand palaces and museums

Home to
San Lorenzo, Porto Antico, Palazzo Rosso

Experience
A ride in an Art Nouveau-style lift to Castelletto for panoramic views of the city

PAGE 104

THE RIVIERA DI LEVANTE

One of the most beautiful coastlines in the whole of Italy, the Riviera di Levante runs from the east of Genoa down to the border of Tuscany in the south. Nestled along wild rocky headlands are delightful sandy coves and quaint fishing villages, the five villages of the Cinque Terre foremost among them. The Levante is home to a number of chic resorts – including Portofino and Rapallo – once the haunt of European aristocrats, now immensely popular with tourists around the world.

Best for
Beautiful rocky coastline and stunning fishing villages

Home to
Cinque Terre, La Spezia, Sarzana, Imperia

Experience
A sunset aperitivo in the Cinque Terre

PAGE 134

THE RIVIERA DI PONENTE

With the city of Genoa at one end and Ventimiglia at the other, the Riviera di Ponente extends for around 150 km (93 miles) in the west of Liguria. The region is a remarkable spot for history lovers, with the prehistoric site of Balzi Rossi and the beautifully preserved medieval centres of Noli and Albenga. Quieter than the Levante, the Ponente's delightful resort towns like Sanremo and Finale Ligure are charming year round, as are the Hanbury Botanic Gardens, which showcase the region's stunning flora.

Best for
Atmospheric medieval centres and prehistoric sites

Home to
Savona, Albenga, Imperia, Dolceacqua

Experience
Exploring the delightful flora on show at Hanbury Botanical Gardens

←

1 The charming fishing village of Boccadasse.

2 Strolling past the Via Garibaldi's imposing palazzi.

3 San Lorenzo's grand columns.

4 Exhibits at Galata Museo di Mare.

The Italian Riviera offers endless options for exploration, from weekends discovering Genoa to longer tours through dramatic coastal landscapes. Wherever you choose to go, our handpicked itineraries will help you plan the perfect trip.

2 DAYS
in Genoa

Day 1

Morning Start the day with a cappuccino and hazelnut-filled "Falstaff" brioche (Giuseppe Verdi's favourite) at Klainguti *(www.botteghestorichegenova.it)*, a Centro Storico bar going strong since 1828. Then wind your way through the *caruggi*, via the cathedral of San Lorenzo *(p60)* and the churches of Il Gesù *(p64)* and San Matteo *(p73)*, up to Via Garibaldi *(p90)*, a Renaissance time capsule. Poke your head into any open doorways of the grand palazzi lining the street as you make for the Musei della Strada Nuova *(p80)*, three palazzi turned into a joint museum (Palazzo Rosso should be your focus). Dip back into the medieval centre for lunch at Sa' Pesta *(sapesta.it)*, a fast-food joint serving *farinata* and vegetable *torte* since medieval times.

Afternoon On the western edge of the city centre is the Villa del Principe *(p88)*, the lavish home of Andrea Doria. It's a staggeringly intimate place that still reverberates with the spirit of the man who single-handedly changed Genoa's history *(p89)*. Walking back to the centre, stop at the Commenda di Pré *(p86)*. Once a medieval hostel for pilgrims, it's now Italy's Museum of Emigration, with emotional testimonies from those who were compelled by poverty to leave.

Evening After your museum tour, enjoy a languorous evening aperitivo at popular bars in the city centre, like Il Mugugno or Ai Troëggi *(p69)*.

Day 2

Morning Start your morning with a stroll round the Porto Antico *(p62)*, to admire how starchitect Renzo Piano transformed a down-at-heel area into a buzzing district. From here, walk along the waterfront to Galata Museo di Mare *(p88)* for a foray into Genoa's maritime history. On the way back, if there's time, call in at the Palazzo Reale *(p87)*, or Royal Palace, whose glittering 17th-century interiors, including a Versailles-style Hall of Mirrors, are fit for a king – even if Genoa never had one.

Afternoon From the Palazzo Reale, pretty Boccadasse *(p100)* is a 70-minute walk; pass through medieval, Renaissance and 19th-century Genoa till you hit the waterfront. Lunch is a cone of fried fish from the food truck overlooking the village. From here, if the weather's good, hop on a bus to Nervi *(p100)*, for a wander around its sprawling parks and jaw-dropping coastal path.

Evening If you're back in the centre before 7pm, grab some chocolates at Romeo Viganotti *(p83)*, before heading for dinner near Piazza Dante.

5 DAYS
on the Riviera di Levante

Day 1

Start off in pretty Camogli *(p125)*, a picture-perfect introduction to the pastel-coloured houses and tiny harbours of the Levante's fishing villages. It's under an hour by train from Genoa.

In the afternoon, once you're finished with the charms of Camogli, take a ferry *(golfoparadiso.it)* around the Portofino peninsula *(p112)*. Stop at San Fruttuoso to visit its Benedictine abbey, which dates back to the 13th century. From there, swap ferry lines *(traghettiportofino.it)* to follow the peninsula round to Portofino, Italy's answer to Saint-Tropez. Escape the crowds with a trip to Castello Brown, a 16th-century clifftop castle saved from ruin by Genoa's former British consul Montague Yeats-Brown; it's a glimpse of Portofino before mass tourism hit. Enjoy a well-deserved spritz and an assortment of nibbles overlooking Oliveri Square in Portofino, before taking an evening ferry ride back to Camogli. The village has several excellent seafood restaurants.

Day 2

Catch the train to Rapallo *(p124)* to spend a leisurely morning admiring the town's Art Nouveau architecture along the seafront, before taking the cable car up to the Santuario di Montallegro. Driving? From Camogli, it's about an hour's drive to the Abbazia di Sant'Andrea di Borzone *(p125)*, one of Italy's oldest Benedictine settlements, in the mountains behind Chiavari. However you spend the morning, arrive by car or train at Moneglia for the afternoon. Another pretty fishing village, it's much quieter than other places on the Riviera di Levante, and has a tranquil beach to unwind on.

Day 3

Set aside two days to truly enjoy everything the Cinque Terre *(p112)* has to offer. If you're travelling by car, it's best to head from Moneglia to La Spezia, and to visit the villages on foot or by train from there. From La Spezia, it's less than ten

1 Sunset over Camogli.
2 The Cinque Terre express.
3 Vernazza's houses.
4 Stone steps in Corniglia.
5 San Giovanni Battista
  in Monterosso.

minutes to Riomaggiore (or 45 minutes by train from Moneglia). The village's houses spill down the sides of a tight cliff-wedged canyon and you can fill your time tackling the 120 km (75 miles) of tracks that crisscross the cliffs and mountainsides. From Riomaggiore, the gentle 1-km (0.5-mile) Via dell'Amore path winds around the cliffs to the equally pretty Manarola. Finish the day in Cantina Capellini's stunning Agrivino bar amid the vines (cantinacapellini.it).

Day 4

A relatively easy hike – flat and then downhill – leads through the vineyards to Corniglia, the middle of the Cinque Terre settlements. Follow the 382 steps down to the train station at the bottom of the village, and stroll along for two minutes to the nearby village of Vernazza. Take a break here, perhaps enjoying a coffee near the quaint marina. From Vernazza, Monterosso al Mare, the largest of the

Cinque Terre towns, is a few minutes away by train. Don't miss the San Giovanni Battista church, with its striking striped facade. Finish the day with a glass of Monterosso's famous limoncino, a cooling lemon liqueur.

Day 5

A 25-minute train ride (or 30-minute drive) south of Monterosso is Luni (p130), home to the most important Roman remains in northern Italy, its buildings and amphitheatre sandwiched between mountain and sea. Nestled in the hills a short walk from the ruins you'll find plenty of spots for a wine-tasting – the Colli di Luni area is well-known for its delightfully crisp whites. Finish your trip at Sarzana (p120), Luni's sophisticated and chic neighbour, only five minutes away by train. It's dominated by the medieval-founded cathedral and fortress, built by powerful ruler Lorenzo de' Medici.

5 DAYS
on the Riviera di Ponente

❚ *Day 1*

Begin in Savona *(p138)* – you'll want a whole day to appreciate the understated loveliness of this sprawling city. Head first to Il Priamàr. There's been a fortress on this spot since Roman times, though this iteration is from the 15th century. Today, it houses two great museums: the Pinacoteca Civica (gallery), with Ligurian works from the Middle Ages onwards, and a modern collection by the likes of Guttuso and De Chirico; and the Civico Museo Storico-Archeologico, whose Arab- and Byzantine-influenced ceramics tell of Liguria's cosmopolitan past. Having spent some time in the museums, wander through Savona's centre to the cathedral.

❚ *Day 2*

A 30-minute drive southwest, nudging inland into the mountains, lie some of Italy's most beautiful caves. The Grotte di Toirano *(p152)* is a network of under-ground cathedral-like karst caverns, wreathed in stalactites, stalagmites and crystal formations. After your 90-minute tour, dip back onto the coast and head west to Albenga *(p148)*, 20 minutes and another world away. Founded by a pre-Roman tribe, its historic centre is one of Liguria's best preserved. You'll need the rest of the day to meander through time, past medieval and Renaissance houses, to the Piazza dei Leoni with its three stone lions, and Palazzo Peloso Cepolla *(p150)*, which houses more than 1,000 Roman amphorae in its Museo Navale Romano. Don't miss the Loggia dei Quattro Canti, which merges Romanesque and Gothic styles, or the 5th-century Baptistery, adorned with mosaics dating back to the Roman Empire.

❚ *Day 3*

From Albenga, it's a 40-minute drive west to Imperia. Make a pit stop in Porto Maurizio, one of two settlements that

1 Il Priamàr fortress in Savona. ↑

2 The small principality of Seborga.

3 The enticing alleys of Porto Maurizio.

4 Grotte di Toirano caves.

5 The Orengo balcony in the Hanbury Botanical Gardens.

make up Imperia, to see Parasio (*p146*), the higher part of town with its winding medieval *caruggi*. Then head for the hills. Dolcedo (*p168*), in Imperia's hinterland, is a river-straddling medieval village, with ancient olive groves carpeting the steep surrounding hills. You'll need to double back and head from the coast into the neighbouring Valle Argentina to Triora (*p169*), another medieval village with the Ligurian Alps rearing up behind. Its ethnographic museum tells the story of Triora's 16th-century witch trials. Stay overnight in nearby Sanremo (*p165*).

Day 4

A half-hour drive inland from Sanremo takes you to the "principality" of Seborga: a quiet village of little more than 300 inhabitants with its own flag, national anthem, currency and monarch. You might think you've imagined it all by the time you reach your next stop: Dolceacqua (*p154*), over in the next valley,

a 40-minute drive. French painter Monet was entranced by this village's medieval beauty; you're here for the local Rossese wine, though, loved by Napoleon.

Day 5

Your final day takes you to Bordighera, a 25-minute drive south of Dolceacqua. Wander the belle époque seafront, and admire cacti in the Giardino Esotico Pallanca (*p168*), before driving 20 minutes west to the sprawling Hanbury Botanical Gardens (*p156*) outside Ventimiglia. Don't miss the Roman theatre, one of the most important Roman sites in Liguria (*p166*). Ventimiglia's ancient church and museum also merit a stop (*p166*), but your priority this afternoon is nearby Balzi Rossi (*p169*), an extraordinary prehistoric site on the French border with finds dating back 240,000 years. Head back to Ventimiglia for a final drink on the delightful promenade.

Pristine Parks

Where parks are concerned, Liguria has an embarrassment of riches. Probably Italy's most famous, the Cinque Terre National Park (p115), is every bit as beautiful as you'd expect, despite the crowds around towns like Vernazza. Other parks you'll have largely to yourself, including the Parco Naturale Regionale di Montemarcello-Magra (p133), the Riviera's only river park, and the forested Parco Naturale Regionale del Beigua (p158), running up to the Piedmont border.

→ Vernazza, surrounded by the hills of the Cinque Terre National Park

THE ITALIAN RIVIERA FOR
NATURAL WONDERS

Liguria's hilly landscapes and undulating coastlines are beautifully untouched. Its many hilltop parks and nature reserves nestle alongside protected beaches and biodiverse waters, making this one of Italy's most glorious regions.

A FRAGILE TERRITORY

The Cinque Terre's vertiginous landscape is vulnerable. Lovingly terraced for over 1,000 years, the cliffsides have been neglected since the mid-1970s, making them unstable, and causing severe landslides. Locals are now working to rebuild the dry stone walls, which are said to rival the Great Wall of China in length.

Glimmering Coastline

Other regions might manicure their coastline into lounger-lined beaches, but Liguria's rocky shores are still surprisingly wild. Portovenere's natural park (p128) wraps around its islands, while the Parco Naturale del Beigua (p158) extends from the mountains and cascades into the sea. In the Portofino Marine Reserve, you can dive down to see the Cristo degli Abissi statue beneath the waves (p111).

→ Looking over the coast from the Bric del Dente, Parco Naturale del Beigua

Fantastic Flora

Liguria's mild climate and gentle coastal winds nurture an assortment of rare plants and flowers. The 44 acres of the Hanbury Botanical Gardens (p156) showcase the beauty of the region's flora, with collections of roses, peonies and citrus plants to admire. In the west of the region, the Riviera dei Fiori, or "Riviera of Flowers", is famous for its fertile soil. Walk the coastline beyond the border of the city of Sanremo (p165) to see rolling olive groves, lush swathes of lavender and fields of swaying buttercups dotting the cliffs.

← A ceiling of blossom at the Hanbury Botanical Gardens

TOP 5 **ECO-FRIENDLY TRAVEL TIPS**

Keep to the path
Protect delicate habitats by sticking to designated trails.

Respect the wildlife
Avoid touching nests or picking rare flowers when walking.

Take care on the cliffs
The cliffs are delicate and prone to landslides; treat them with care.

Leave no trace
Ensure all rubbish is properly disposed of.

Take public transport
Avoid congestion in the high season by taking the bus or train.

The mountains looming above Aveto Natural Regional Park ↑

Soaring Mountains

Liguria's mountains have long protected its people from marauders. Monte Aiona rears 1,700 m (5,600 ft) above the Aveto Natural Regional Park (p125), with trails leading to the summit, while Monte Beigua (p158) offers stunning sea views. The best way to roam the mountains is by lacing up your hiking boots and following the Alta Via dei Monti Liguri trail (p158).

Coastal Hikes

With a plethora of way-marked trails crisscrossing the region, there's no better way to explore this coastline than on foot. The Cinque Terre National Park (p115) has roughly 120 km (75 miles) of trails to explore, the most famous of which is the Sentiero Azzuro (Blue Path), which connects the area's five villages. Feeling fit? Tackle the 600-km (375-mile) Sentiero Liguria, a stunning long distance hiking trail that traces the wild Ligurian coast, from the small town of Grimaldi to Luni (p130).

$\rightarrow$

Walking the Sentiero Azzuro through the Cinque Terre

THE ITALIAN RIVIERA FOR
COASTAL ADVENTURES

Stretching for 350 km (220 miles), Liguria's coastline encompasses an array of coves, caves and beaches. From cycling along the beaches to taking a leisurely swim, there's something for every taste on this varied waterfront.

Beautiful Beaches

When all that cycling, snorkelling and walking makes you weary, you can kick back on the to-die-for beaches you'll see at every turn. The Portofino peninsula (p108) is home to some of the region's most blissful sands: try Baia di Paraggi (p110), near Paraggi, for a perfect snapshot of Ligurian beach culture. Even Genoa has a city beach at the dinky cove of Boccadasse (p100).

$\leftarrow$

Loungers lining the beach on the Portofino peninsula

COASTAL STROLLS

Genoa to Boccadasse
Walk 3.5-km (2-miles)
from Genoa to charming
Boccadasse (p100).

**San Lorenzo al Mare
to Cavi**
It's a 5-km (3-mile) stroll
along the beach to the
village of Cavi.

Camogli to San Rocco
Explore Portofino (p108)
with a 5-km (3-mile)
walk to San Rocco.

Via dell'Amore
Stroll the Cinque Terre's
verdant hills (p116).

Boat Trips

Every town offers boat trips:
some reveal a well-known
spot from a new angle, while
others involve excursions to
remote areas, including Isola
Gallinara (p149). Navigazione
Golfo dei Poeti (navigazione-
golfodeipoeti.it) offers routes
around La Spezia, Porto
Venere and Vernazza.

→

A ferry cruise from the
stunning town
of Vernazza

Sea Sports

The unique topography of Liguria - with its
tiny coves, caves and reefs teeming with
sea life - makes the area perfect for water
sports. The protected waters of the
Portofino peninsula offer spectacular
diving. Try diving down to the Cristo degli
Abissi statue (p111), or kayaking in the
Golfo dei Poeti from Lerici (p132).

→

Kayakers in the wild
waves near Lerici

Explore Food Festivals

In towns across the region, food festivals provide an irresistible glimpse into Liguria's culinary heritage. Top of them all is the Sagra del Pesce in Camogli (p122), held on the second Sunday of May, during which around three tons of fresh, locally caught fish are fried in huge pans. Every August, Toirano hosts the Festa dei Gumbi, its medieval streets filled with stalls hawking traditional dishes, including stuffed and fried vegetables, *panissa*, meat and seafood.

→

Chefs preparing fresh fish at Sagra del Pesce in Camogli

THE ITALIAN RIVIERA FOR
FOODIES

If you think Italian food is defined by tomato sauce and pizza, you're in for a delightful surprise. Separated from the rest of Italy by mountains, Liguria's food culture is as much influenced by foreign medieval trade routes as it is by neighbouring regions, with dishes you won't find anywhere else.

Savour the Pesto

Liguria's pasta sauces are raw and nut-based, with pesto the most famous of all. In Genoa, World Pesto Championships finalist Enrica Monzani will teach you how to make it in her kitchen (asmallkitchenin genoa.com), or you can learn with chefs at Nessun Dorma in Manarola (nessundorma-cinqueterre.com).

Did You Know?

Ligurian pesto is made with garlic from the Valle Arroscia, which is noted for its intense aroma and flavour.

↑ Making traditional Ligurian pesto, with fresh basil and crunchy pine nuts

Sample Historic Delicacies

From treats usually served at sea to ingredients brought back from distant shores, many Ligurian dishes are influenced by Genoa's maritime history. Focaccia is now enjoyed globally, but it was first served in Liguria as a variation of the unleavened bread eaten throughout the Middle East. Then there's *cappon magro*, a pyramid of vegetables and fish on a sea biscuit, or *torte di verdura* – delectable vegetable pies.

←

Fresh focaccia dotted with black olives

Take a Foodie Tour of Genoa

Genoa is arguably the capital of Italian street food, and the city's finest treats – like *panissa* (chickpea strips) and *frisceu* (dough balls) – are best served from a small hatch or stall. Do Eat Better Experience *(doeatbetter experience.com)* offers no fewer than three Genoa food tours – traditional, gourmet and street food – while Enrica Monzani picks out the best holes-in-the-wall in the *caruggi* on her food tours *(asmallkitcheningenoa.com)*.

→

Queueing for street food at a popular food hatch in Genoa's Centro Storico

---

💬 INSIDER TIP
Ligurian Anchovies

Anchovies are a staple of Ligurian cuisine. Look out for the breaded and stuffed variety, served as an appetizer in many Genoese restaurants. They pair perfectly with a glass of local white wine.

Craft Brews

Despite the region's wine heritage, local craft beer is deservedly popular. Sassello, the headquarters of the Parco Naturale del Beigua *(p158)*, is home to El Issor brewery *(birrificioelissor.com)* and Birrificio Altavia *(birrificio-altavia.it)*; the latter has a tap room in summer and a bustling outlet in Savona year-round. Birrificio del Golfo *(birrificiodelgolfo.com)* in La Spezia *(p118)* has a sea salt-spiced beer – it's a unique and unmistakably coastal tipple.

↑ Refreshing lager served al fresco, a perfect accompaniment to pizza

THE ITALIAN RIVIERA
BY THE GLASS

Liguria's steep cliffs and rolling mountains make for delightful tiered vineyards, and for centuries hardy locals have terraced the undulating landscape. The result? A delectable assortment of wines. Beer and spirit lovers are also well catered for, with superb breweries and tasty liqueurs.

World-class Wines

Sea-sprayed cliffs produce intensely mineral, saline whites that instantly transport you to the coast. One of the best places to start is at the Durin winery *(durin.it)*, near Savona, which ages sparkling wines in the caves of Toirano *(p152)*. Cantine Lunae *(cantinelunae.com)*, in the Colli di Luni DOC area, pairs local cured meats with its wines between the vines at its lavish 18th-century farmhouse *(calunae.com)*.

6,000
___
The number of hectares (14,800 acres) of vineyard across the wider Ligurian region.

Aperitivo in the Alleys

Genoa *(p54)* is home to two famous drinks. Corochinato vermouth is a local white wine fortified with 20-odd herbs and spices, including cinchona bark, absinthe and oregano, in a winning blend that's been going strong since 1886. Camatti is a century-old *amaro* voted best in the world in 2023. They're ideally consumed in the *caruggi* during aperitivo hour – try them at bars like Il Mugugno *(ilmugugnogenovese.it)* and Ai Troëggi *(p69)*.

↑ Ai Troëggi bar in the bustling heart of Genoa

Drinking Cinque Terre

In the medieval period, Cinque Terre wines graced the tables of popes and kings. Today, after decades of abandonment, the scene is blossoming again. Try a glass of Cinque Terre DOC at Cantina Capellini's vineyard bar *(cantinacapellini.it)*, or hike for a tasting with views over Vernazza at Cheo *(cheo.it)*.

←

A selection of local Cinque Terre wines

TOP 4 LOCAL WINES TO SAMPLE

Sciacchetrà
This white wine has been produced since the Middle Ages.

Cinque Terre DOC
A quality local wine produced high in the hills of Cinque Terre.

Rossese
This Dolceacqua grape was Napoleon's pick.

Colli di Luni DOC
The fine wine produced around La Spezia falls under the Colli di Luni DOC.

←

The rolling hills and lush vineyards near Dolceacqua

Marvellous Museums

Genoa is home to world-class museums exploring everything from natural history to Asian art. Highlights include the conjoined Musei di Strada Nuova *(p80)* in Genoa, housed in sumptuous palazzi, and Galata Museo del Mare *(p88)*, which tells the incredible story of Italian emigration.

←

Nautical exhibits on display at the Museo del Mare in Genoa

THE ITALIAN RIVIERA FOR
ART AND CULTURE

From Byron to Verdi, artists of various disciplines have always flocked to Liguria, often using the spectacular landscape as a muse. Today, their creative legacy runs deep throughout the region, and its towns and villages play host to numerous concerts, festivals and exhibitions.

Literary Connections

British writers have had a special connection with Liguria since the days of the Grand Tour, and the Gulf of Lerici is today known as the Gulf of Poets *(p118)*. English poet Lord Byron stayed in Albaro *(p100)* and visited fellow writers Mary and Percy Bysshe Shelley. Poetry lovers can walk Shelley's Path to Casa Magni *(p132)*, near Lerici, where the Shelleys lived and wrote. Later writers, including D H Lawrence and Virginia Woolf, flocked to San Terenzo, while Italian writer Italo Calvino wove Sanremo *(p165)*, his parents' city, into his works. Visit Piazza Nota in the centre to see a plaque marking where Calvino studied as a young man.

→

The church of San Pietro overlooking the vast and beautiful Gulf of Poets

Festival Culture

Music fans should head to the Sanremo Music Festival, the inspiration for Eurovision. Held every February since 1951, it's the longest-running televised music competition. Other local arts festivals include Sestri Levante's Andersen Festival; held in June, it explores theatre.

$\rightarrow$

Performers lighting up the stage at the Sanremo Music Festival

Classical Highs

Genoa wasn't only an economic powerhouse in its heyday, it was also a thriving centre of classical music, with the iconic Teatro Carlo Felice *(p66)* hosting operatic performances from the world's best. But classical culture is not confined to the city: the superb Nervi *(p101)* Music Ballet Festival starts in late June.

$\leftarrow$

The auditorium of the world renowned Teatro Carlo Felice

THE SHELLEYS IN THE RIVIERA

English writers Mary Shelley and Percy Bysshe Shelley lived in splendid isolation in an old house called Casa Magni in 1822, and anchored their sailing boat in Lerici. They were both profoundly inspired by the landscapes of the Riviera. On 8 July 1822, as he was returning to Lerici from nearby Livorno in his boat, Percy Bysshe Shelley was caught in a sudden storm in the gulf and drowned. His corpse would wash up on the beach at Viareggio, where he was cremated. The story has become an iconic piece of local lore, and contributes to the area's mystery.

Explore Quieter Coasts

No Ligurian beach is empty in summer, but with over 300 km (200 miles) of coastline, there's plenty to go around. Moneglia is peaceful, as is Noli (p160) – both towns' beaches regularly make Blue Flag lists for sustainability. Heading south, take a ferry from La Spezia or Portovenere to quiet Cala del Pozzale, on the west side of Palmaria island (p129). Up for a hike? Down a steep, 700-step path from Montemarcello (p133), the hidden sands of Punta Corva await. You'll often have the spot to yourself.

$\rightarrow$

A quiet beach nestled beneath hills near the town of Noli

THE ITALIAN RIVIERA
OFF THE
BEATEN TRACK

While visitors flock to the resorts in summer, inland Liguria remains a quieter place of forested mountains, tranquil valleys and ancient villages. The region's vast and varied terrain means that even in the busiest season, pockets of calm can always be found nearby.

↑ The old town of Ameglia, with the Apuan Alps rising behind

Head Inland

Take to the hills to find villages that haven't changed in centuries. Towards the Tuscan border, time stands still in the village of Ameglia (p130), with a knot of winding alleys offering stunning views over the Apuan Alps. The deep valleys around the village of Santo Stefano d'Aveto (p124) seem a world away from Liguria's coastal hotspots, enclosed by vast mountains and forests of Norway spruce. On the Ponente side is the medieval village of Dolceacqua (p154), home to Rossese wine; Monet's paintings of the village highlight its beauty.

Go West

For a truly restorative trip, head west of Genoa along the Riviera del Ponente, where fewer visitors tread. Away from the Levante's big-hitter attractions like Portofino and Cinque Terre, you'll find the calm and expansive greenery of Parco Naturale Regionale del Beigua (p158), laidback towns like Pieve di Teco (p165), and small and endlessly charming beach resorts like Laigueglia (p163) and Andora (p164).

$\leftarrow$

The splendid coastal resort of Laigueglia

Linger in Genoa

With an array of stunning landscapes on its doorstep, Genoa is often seen as a gateway to the Riviera di Levante, and many visitors swiftly pass through. This means the tiered city never feels overcrowded, and you might even have sights like the Villa del Principe (p88) or the Palazzo Rosso (p80) to yourselves. To soak it all in, walk the alleyways early in the morning and admire the sunrise over the sumptuous palazzi on Via Garibaldi (p90).

$\rightarrow$

The beautiful frescoes adorning the halls of Genoa's Villa del Principe

---

💬 INSIDER TIP
The Low Season

Visit the Riviera between November and March to find an altogether quieter region. Though the climate is mild all year, snow is known to cover the hills in winter.

Riding the Rails

These aren't your average train rides. The narrow-gauge railway from Genoa to Casella *(p101)* climbs from city to mountain, traversing tunnels, viaducts and forested cliffsides as it goes, and dropping you off in prime position for hiking and cycling trails. Then there's the Cinque Terre Express from La Spezia to Levanto, which rolls slowly through the Cinque Terre National Park *(p114)*. Most of Liguria's train routes hug the coast, with the sparkling sea views only stopping as you hit the (many) tunnels.

THE ITALIAN RIVIERA FOR
SCENIC JOURNEYS

The Riviera's swoon-worthy natural landscapes and grand historic buildings are the perfect backdrop for long journeys. Whether it's on a coast-hugging train ride, a scenic cycling route or even public transport within the cities, there's always something to look at when travelling through Liguria.

On the Water

Seeing the Ligurian coastline from the water brings home its unique beauty, revealing the precipitous drops and mountains with villages nestled at their base. Take a spin around the Portovenere archipelago to Palmaria, Tino and Tinetto *(p128)*, or start from La Spezia and tour the Golfo dei Poeti or the Cinque Terre. Boats from Alassio and Imperia loop around Isola Gallinara *(p149)*, a remote coastal nature reserve perfect for snorkelling.

←

The stunning waters of the Golfo dei Poeti lapping the harbour of Lerici

← The Casella train traversing the cliffs near Genoa

> 📷 PICTURE PERFECT
> **City Skyline**
>
> From the upper balcony of the Castelletto lift, you can photograph Genoa's famous slate roofs set against a backdrop of medieval towers and Baroque facades, all rising before the distant ocean. There are few more iconic images of the city.

Climbing High

No fewer than 12 public lifts knit Genoa's layers together, whisking you from one era to the next. The Castelletto lift *(p85)* is the most beautiful, with sweeping views of the medieval city, while the Sant'Anna funicular drops you near the Antica Farmacia Sant'Anna. In Rapallo *(p124)*, a cable car lifts you to the grand Santuario di Montallegro for a sublime coastal panorama.

→ Genoa's grand palazzi seen from the balcony of the Castelletto lift

On Two Wheels

New cycle trails are always opening around the Riviera, testament to the appeal of exploring by bike. An old train track on the Riviera di Ponente is now a 24-km (15-mile) cycle track *(p170)*, running from Diano Marina to Ospedaletti, passing six villages. And then there's Cinque Terre *(p115)* – while the park is famous for its hiking, it has seven cycling routes.

→ The Pista Ciclabile track running through the Riviera di Ponente

Medieval Mazes

The medieval heyday of the Genoese Republic is visible at every turn. The streets of the beautifully preserved town of Albenga (p148) are dotted with lofty towers; their height was traditionally a symbol of their owner's wealth. Other towns have intact medieval quarters, like Imperia's Parasio (p146) and the alleys of Levanto, while in the mountains you'll find medieval villages such as Triora and Taggia (p168.

→

Medieval towers in the ancient centre of Albenga

THE ITALIAN RIVIERA FOR
ARCHITECTURE

From medieval to Gothic, high Baroque to defiantly modern, Liguria's architecture tells the story of its immensely wealthy past and ultra-chic present. The region's precipitous terrain, meanwhile, has long prompted architects to devise unique statement structures.

Military Structures

Many towns are dominated by castles or forts, designed to protect the region from ocean-crossing marauders. Savona's Il Priamàr (p138) was built on a promontory in 1542 and now houses the city's first archaeological museum. Cervo's castle (p164) - with its thick stone walls and four towers - is a fine example of Ligurian military architecture from the Middle Ages. Perhaps the most spectacular is Castello Brown in Portofino (p108), which dates back to 1425, with new garrisons and barracks added throughout the following centuries.

→

Castello Brown in Portofino looming over the green hills

Genoa's Layers

Genoa is an architectural lasagne, layered with buildings from the medieval period to the early 20th century. Start in the warrens of the Centro Storico, where Romanesque churches such as Santo Stefano *(p66)* and the jewel box of San Pietro in Banchi *(p71)* are squashed between medieval alleys. Higher up, dip into the doorways of Renaissance mansions on Via Garibaldi – don't miss Palazzo Rosso *(p80)* – before ascending to Castelletto's *(p85)* elegant 20th-century mansions.

↑ Grand Renaissance palazzi along Genoa's Via Garibaldi

Holy Lands

Amid the valleys and cliffside crags of Liguria lie ancient churches, from the Romanesque San Paragorio in Noli *(p161)*, which dates back to the 6th century, to Portovenere's San Pietro, cantilevered over the sea *(p128)*. The cathedral of Santa Maria Assunta in Sarzana *(p120)* was started in 1204 and completed two centuries later.

←

Portovenere's San Pietro church perched on a crag above the waves

Genoa for All Ages

Few cities cater for children quite like Genoa. Renzo Piano might as well have designed the city's Porto Antico *(p62)* for families, since every inch of it, from the Bigo lift to the eye-catching Biosphere and the world-class Aquarium, is kid-friendly. The Città dei Bambini museum *(p63)*, with a range of scientific and educational exhibits and activities, is specifically created for the under-12s.

→

Renzo Piano's Porto Antico, with its array of family-friendly attractions

THE ITALIAN RIVIERA FOR
FAMILIES

Beaches, gelato and that child-friendly Italian attitude – the Riviera is one of the country's most perfect regions for a memorable family holiday. Many of the greatest attractions were designed with children in mind, so you'll never be stuck for places to take the little ones.

Making Travel Fun

Are we there yet? Hope not! Getting around is fun in Liguria, with hillside towns like Rapallo offering thrilling cable car ascents *(p124)* and boat rides up for grabs at every beach. On dry land, the Cinque Terre Express route *(p112)* – slow trains calling at all five of the villages – is gorgeous, and the service offers discounts for families and children. While in Portofino, hire a sturdy sailing boat from a local company like Giorgio Mussini *(giorgiomussini.com)* and sail the tranquil coast-line. The kids will love jumping into the shallow azure waters.

←

Travelling by train between the five towns of the Cinque Terre

Going Underground

Older kids will relish getting to know Liguria's vertiginous landscape from the inside, with a trip to its caves. See the underground lakes at the Grotte di Borgio Verezzi (p162), and make out weird and wonderful shapes in the stalactites and stalagmites of the Grotte di Toirano (p152).

← Startling stalactites in the Grotte di Borgio Verezzi

INSIDER TIP
Family Hikes

Given the region's rough terrain, many hikes are unsuitable for younger children. The route between Vernazza and Monterosso (p116), however, is flat and safe for both pushchairs and less confident walkers.

Kid-friendly Food

Even the fussiest eaters will find lots to love in Liguria. From beachside gelato to pesto pasta, as well as pizza at every turn, the food here is as fun as the towns' rainbow-coloured houses. Speaking of those houses, Pontorosso, the town in Disney Pixar's film *Luca* (2021), was inspired by Vernazza (p114).

↑ Refreshing with an ice cream in the town of Vernazza

A YEAR IN
THE ITALIAN
RIVIERA

JANUARY

△ **Festa di Capodanno** *(New Year's Eve)*. See in the New Year with fireworks, costumes and music in Liguria's capital, Genoa.
Carnevale di Loano *(end Jan–end Feb)*. Liguria's largest carnival takes place in Loano.

FEBRUARY

Festa dei Furgari *(early Feb)*. Held since 1626, Furgari sees huge bonfires lit across Taggia.
△ **Sanremo Music Festival** *(late Feb)*. Held since 1951, this is the longest-running televized music competition.

MAY

△ **Sagra del Pesce** *(early May)*. This celebration of the ocean's bounty sees fish fried in huge pans in Camogli's central square.
Monterosso Lemon Festival *(mid-May)*. A festival giving thanks for Liguria's favourite fruit, with lemon producers selling their wares.

JUNE

The Genoa International Poetry Festival *(early June)*. Make the most of Liguria's literary heritage at this celebration of verse, with numerous readings.
△ **Slow Fish festival** *(mid-June)*. The Slow Fish festival in Genoa sees a host of conferences and events focused on sustainability and local health.

SEPTEMBER

Festa della Donna della Villa, Ceriana *(6 Sep)*. The celebrations in honour of the Madonna della Villa feature a night-time torchlight procession.
△ **Regata Storica dei Rioni** *(late Sept)*. A huge procession winds through the streets of Noli during this regatta.

OCTOBER

Genoa Science Festival *(late Oct)*. This major international scientific event features numerous talks and interactive displays.
△ **Salone Internazionale della Nautica** *(late Oct)*. Genoa's international boat show brings thousands of nautical enthusiasts.

MARCH

Fiera di San Giuseppe *(late March)*. This three-day fair in La Spezia celebrates local food, with a range of family-friendly events and talks.

△ **Milano–Sanremo Race** *(first Sat after 19 Mar)*. A classic long-distance cycling race with a rich and illustrious history.

APRIL

Semana Santa *(late March/early April)*. Liguria celebrates with Easter pageantry during Holy Week.

△ **Euroflora** *(April–May)*. The largest exhibition of flowers and plants in the world, held every five years, with the next held in Genoa (Nervi) in 2025.

Rolli Days *(throughout April)*. In Genoa, the grand palazzi open free to the public on certain days throughout the month.

JULY

Feast of Sant'Erasmo *(last Sunday in July)*. To celebrate the feast of Sant'Erasmo, an effigy of the saint is carried out to sea and placed on a traditional boat, a *gussu*.

△ **Cristo degli Abissi** *(late July)* Every year in honour of all those who died at sea, a mystical and engaging ceremony takes place near the statue of Cristo degli Abissi in San Fruttuoso.

AUGUST

Torta dei Fieschi *(mid-Aug)*. A huge procession of floats culminates in the ceremonial slicing of an enormous cake in Lavagna.

△ **Festa della Madonna Bianca** *(17 Aug)*. Admire Portovenere illuminated by thousands of lanterns draped around the bay on the celebration of the White Madonna.

NOVEMBER

Olioliva *(early Nov)*. This event is dedicated to olive oil, with local purveyors offering samples of their wares in Imperia.

△ **Pane e Olio** *(early Nov)*. See in the region's olive harvest with workshops for adults and children, cooking shows, exhibitions and visits to olive groves and oil mills in Sestri Levante.

DECEMBER

Natale Subacqueo *(24 Dec)* The underwater nativity in Tellaro is one of the oldest and most evocative Christmas events in Liguria, with nativity scenes staged in the waters around the ancient church of San Giorgio.

△ **La Fiera di Natale** *(Dec to mid-Jan)*. Genoa's Christmas fair brings decorative nativity scenes, vast markets offering local wares and a host of carol services throughout the city.

A BRIEF
HISTORY

With mountains slicing it off from the Italian peninsula, Liguria has always looked outwards. Its ancient peoples engaged in business with Mediterranean powerhouses before Genoa's oligarchs made the region a centre of finance. Today, the Riviera maintains a thriving tourist industry.

The Prehistoric Riviera

The mild climate and deep waters of the northwest coast of what is now Italy have lured humans for hundreds of thousands of years. Its cliffs doubled as prehistoric housing: the caves at Balzi Rossi were inhabited from the Palaeolithic age – the tombs there have been dated to 240,000 years ago – while Neanderthal remains have been found in the Toirano caves. Traces of *Homo sapiens* have been found at both sites.

① A map of Genoa, dated 1608.

② Lithograph of the Grotte di Toirano caves.

③ A Roman bridge built in Albenga.

④ The view of Genoa's harbour in 1481, by Genoese artist Cristoforo Grassi (1565-1598).

Timeline of events

350,000 BCE
Palaeolithic tribes use stone tools in the hills above Finale Ligure.

240,000 BCE
The Balzi Rossi caves are used as a burial site.

12,340 BCE
Handprints and footprints found in the Grotte di Toirano caves.

177 BCE
The Romans found Portus Lunae (Luni).

200 BCE-100 CE
Roman authors including Cato and Livy mention Ligurian tribes in their writings.

Early Years

Liguria gets its name from the *Liguri*, or Ligurians, pre-Roman people that occupied modern Liguria as well as parts of Piedmont, Tuscany and the Maritime Alps. They founded the small settlement of Genoa in the fifth or fourth millennium BCE, and the population grew fast.

The Ligurian people didn't take well to the Romans, who were rapidly expanding their empire, and Ligurian tribes fought fiercely, with those in Genoa a notable exception – the settlement was willingly incorporated into the Roman empire in the 2nd century BCE.

Emerging Power

Rome gradually conquered the rest of Liguria, establishing the Via Postumia – a route from Genoa to Lombardy and Veneto – in 148 BCE. Around 1000 CE, following centuries of occupation by the Byzantines, Franks and others, Liguria's city states came into their own. Their activities revolved around maritime trade, with the (unofficial) republic of Genoa emerging as a mercantile force. By the 15th century, it was a Mediterranean superpower.

Did You Know?

Genoese ships from Noli and Savona played a vital role in the Crusades, emphasizing the city's naval power.

538 CE
The Byzantines conquer Liguria.

1097 CE
Genoa contributes galleys to the First Crusade.

1284
Genoa trounces Pisa at the Battle of Meloria and Venice at Korčula in 1298.

1238 CE
Albenga, Savona and Ventimiglia form a short-lived alliance against Genoa.

1339
Genoa elects its first doge.

1

2

The City of Miracles

In 1528, Andrea Doria – a captain and statesman from one of Genoa's most powerful families – allied with Spain, signing a deal for the city's bankers to finance the Spanish crown as it colonized the Americas. The deal led to unthinkable wealth for Genoa, lending it the nickname *"la città dei miracoli"* – the city of miracles. Newly minted oligarchs built a new city on top of the medieval core, constructing lavish palaces along the Strade Nuove. In 1576, the republic created a *rollo* (list) of mansions fit for VIP visitors. Nearly 90 of these "Palazzi dei Rolli" still exist.

Republic of (French) Liguria

Too busy revelling in its sizable wealth, Genoa's military prowess had weakened towards the end of the 16th century. The French attacked unsuccessfully in 1684, but finally took control a century later, when French military commander Napoleon Bonaparte arrived in Italy. Napoleon established the Republic of Liguria in 1797; though the republic retained much of its independence, it became part of the broader Napoleonic empire in 1805.

GENOA'S DOGES

The enterprising trading activities of Genoa's great ship-owning families like the Dorias turned the city into a true power from the beginning of the 12th century. At this time, the city was governed by powerful doges, selected by wealthy families and appointed for life. They maintained relatively peaceful rule until the Napoleonic Wars.

Timeline of events

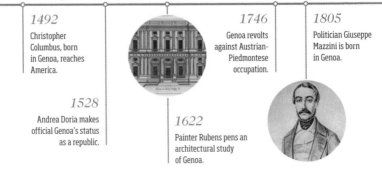

1492
Christopher Columbus, born in Genoa, reaches America.

1528
Andrea Doria makes official Genoa's status as a republic.

1622
Painter Rubens pens an architectural study of Genoa.

1746
Genoa revolts against Austrian-Piedmontese occupation.

1805
Politician Giuseppe Mazzini is born in Genoa.

After Napoleon's defeat at Waterloo in 1815, the Congress of Vienna – which parcelled out his former dominions – assigned Liguria to the house of Savoy, enfolding it into the Kingdom of Sardinia-Piedmont. Genoa became the main port for the landlocked Piedmontese, who constructed a new port, enlarged it twice, and brought in its top architects to add another "'new'" town, running on from the Strade Nuove, with new buildings including the Teatro Carlo Felice.

The Road to Unification

Liguria resented Piedmontese rule, and the Risorgimento movement, which sought a unified Italy, put down roots in the region, where its leader Giuseppe Mazzini was born. Italian general and republican Giuseppe Garibaldi's troops set sail for the south of Italy from Quarto (today a suburb of Genoa) in 1860, successfully unifying the north and south of the country a year later. The city of Genoa became the new country's major port; along with Naples, it also became the main departure route for emigrants driven out of Italy by poverty. Nearly 19 million Italians left for good between 1861 and 1985.

① Naval captain and politician Andrea Doria. ↑

② Watercolour showing the port of Genoa (1878).

③ Map highlighting the Kingdom of Sardinia-Piedmont.

④ Garibaldi and his republicans embarking in Quarto, near Genoa, before heading south.

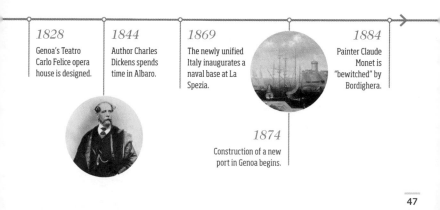

1828
Genoa's Teatro Carlo Felice opera house is designed.

1844
Author Charles Dickens spends time in Albaro.

1869
The newly unified Italy inaugurates a naval base at La Spezia.

1884
Painter Claude Monet is "bewitched" by Bordighera.

1874
Construction of a new port in Genoa begins.

Post-War Rebirth

Liguria's coastal railway network did wonders for 19th-century tourism, but the region's lines and ports were pummelled in World War II. Genoa was badly bombed; dubious postwar reconstruction included the infamous *sopraelevata*, or elevated highway, which slashes across the seafront. The industrial future looked bright, however: Italy was now a republic, and Turin's car factories shipped their wares from Genoa, while Savona and La Spezia were also booming. In the 1960s, new motorways connected the coast; a road was built from La Spezia to Levanto, modernizing the Cinque Terre.

Genoa's Fortunes

By the 1990s, Genoa was often dismissed as a declining port. Everything changed when it hosted Expo 1992, a world fair themed around the 500th anniversary of Genoese explorer Christopher Columbus reaching America. In anticipation of Expo, architect Renzo Piano transformed the down-at-heel Porto Antico into a thriving new neighbourhood. The city went on to host the 27th G8 summit in 2001, but the event marked

↑ The new motorway built in 1960, connecting La Spezia and Levanto

Timeline of events

1941-2
Genoa is repeatedly blitzed by the Allies.

1945
Ventimiglia is occupied by France at the end of the war.

1951
The Sanremo Music Festival is born.

1954
The Cristo degli Abissi statue is installed underwater off San Fruttuoso.

1958
Singer Fred Buscaglione records "I Found my Love in Portofino".

the crescendo of the worldwide anti-globalization protests. Genoa's police force met protestors with fierce brutality, leaving 400 injured and killing one. The city worked hard to move beyond this dark episode, and investment in its cultural sector led to Genoa becoming European Capital of Culture in 2004.

Liguria Today

In 2011, major flooding in the Cinque Terre killed 13 and devastated the village of Vernazza. Just a few years later, in 2018, the Morandi motorway bridge in Genoa collapsed, killing 43 and plunging Liguria into a year-long state of emergency. Renzo Piano designed its replacement, which opened in 2020.

These tragedies led to a prolonged feeling of despondency in the region, but the Riviera is now thriving once again, due largely to the sizeable influence of its tourism sector. Though the very real issue of overtourism pushes more locals away from the coast, global visitors remain the primary driver of the local economy. The region's popularity shows no signs of waning: Genoa and La Spezia are bustling cruise ports, Cinque Terre is Italy's most-visited national park, and a vast new waterfront for eastern Genoa will debut in December 2024.

1 Railway arches in Genoa are blitzed during World War II.

2 Genoa's Porto Antico, newly transformed by Renzo Piano in 1992.

3 The collapse of the Morandi motorway bridge in 2018.

4 Visitors walk the popular Cinque Terre hiking trails.

1989
A poignant Monument to the Emigrant is unveiled in remote Favale di Malvaro.

1997
Cinque Terre is declared a UNESCO World Heritage site.

2022
Savona welcomes refugees from its twin city, Ukraine's Mariupol.

2021
Disney's animated film *Luca* recreates Vernazza and Portofino on screen.

2023
The Ocean Race picks Genoa as its finishing line.

EXPERIENCE
GENOA

The arches of Genoa's San Lorenzo

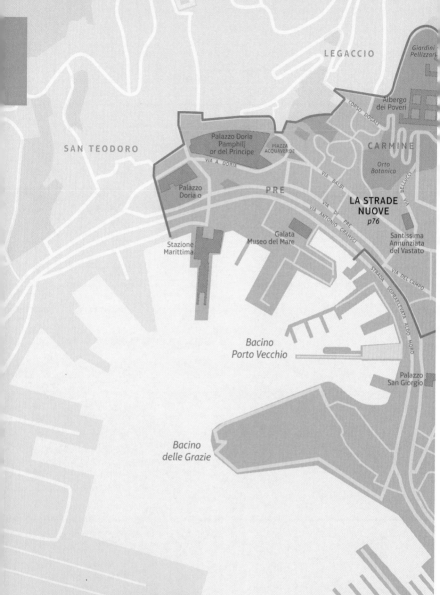

LEGACCIO

Giardini Pellizzari

Albergo dei Poveri

CORSO DOGALI

SAN TEODORO

Palazzo Doria Pamphilj or del Principe

PIAZZA ACQUAVERDE

VIA A. DORIA

CARMINE

Orto Botanico

VIA PALBI

Palazzo Doria o

PRE

LA STRADE NUOVE
p76

VIA DI PRE

VIA ANTONIO GRAMSCI

VIA BELLUCCI

Stazione Marittima

Galata Museo del Mare

Santissima Annunziata del Vastato

VIA DEL CAMPO

VIA XX SETTEMBRE

STRADA SOPRAELEVATA ALDO MORO

Bacino Porto Vecchio

Palazzo San Giorgio

Bacino delle Grazie

EXPLORE
GENOA

This guide divides Genoa into three
sightseeing areas: the two on this map and
one for sights beyond the city centre. Find out
more about each area on the following pages.

LOCATOR MAP

LOMBARDY

PIEDMONT

EMILIA-
ROMAGNA

LIGURIA

GENOA

RIVIERA DI
PONENTE

RIVIERA DI
LEVANTE

*Ligurian
Sea*

CASTELLETTO

MADDALENA

PALAZZO
BIANCO

Palazzo
Spinola

San Siro

Museo di Arte
Orientale Edoardo
Chiossone

Palazzo
Doria

Monumento
"G. Mazzini"

PIAZZA
BANCHI

Teatro
Carlo Felice

San
Lorenzo

MOLO

Palazzo
Ducale

VIA XX SETTEMBRE

PIAZZA
DELLE ERBE

PORTONA

Museo di
Sant'Agostino

IL CENTRO
STORICO
p56

*Giardini
Baltimora*

Museo Civico di
Storia Naturale
Giacomo Doria

Basilica di
Santa Maria
Assunta in
Carignano

CARIGNANO

Contemporary
Art Museum of
Villa Croce

0 metres   450

0 yards   450

N

GETTING TO KNOW
GENOA

Originally built around the coast, Genoa rapidly expanded upwards into the hills. A labyrinth of medieval *caruggi*, Liguria's narrow alleys, leads up the steep slopes behind the port, followed by new streets laid out in the 16th and 17th centuries, with modern quarters at the city's highest point.

PAGE 56

IL CENTRO STORICO

The old heart of Genoa is grouped around Porto Antico, a lively harbour redesigned by architect Renzo Piano in the 1990s. The port is linked to a warren of alleyways which connect the area's numerous public squares. Largely pedestrianized due to the narrow streets, the old centre is home to some of the city's finest buildings, including San Lorenzo and the Teatro Carlo Felice.

Best for
Baroque architecture and grand galleries

Home to
Porto Antico, San Lorenzo

Experience
Strolling the dense alleys and grand squares

LE STRADE NUOVE

The district known as Le Strade Nuove ("new streets") houses the Via Garibaldi, a grand thoroughfare bordered by the city's most remarkable palazzi. Many of these grand Baroque and Renaissance buildings now comprise a UNESCO World Heritage site, and former private residences house museums and galleries, the highlight being the joint museum known as Musei di Strade Nuove. Walking through the new streets reveals the immense wealth and culture of the city.

Best for
Museums and stately palazzi

Home to
Palazzo Rosso

Experience
Genoa's affluence on a tour of Via Garibaldi

BEYOND THE CENTRE

Though there is more than enough to keep you occupied in Genoa's bustling centre, head beyond the central streets and old alleys to find suburbs of great variety. The steep landscape and beautiful coastline that border the city offer a host of medieval gems, such as the church of San Siro di Struppa with its rolling gardens and lush vineyards. The residential district of Albaro is home to pretty villas, while the delightful resort of Noli is rich in Art Nouveau splendour.

Best for
Tranquil coastlines and medieval churches

Home to
Parco Durazzo Pallavicini

Experience
Relaxing on the beach in the chic resort of Nervi

Charming Piazza delle Erbe in Genoa's old town

IL CENTRO STORICO

The historic centre and ancient heart of Genoa stretches back from the port, with a maze of medieval *caruggi* (alleyways) forming a hilly network of piazzas, streets and staircases. The Centro Storico is Europe's largest medieval centre, its grand buildings showcasing a striking mix of architectural styles, from the 14th-century walls to the high Baroque piazzas. As Genoa's thriving maritime industries flourished prior to the 16th century, the Centro Storico became the social heart of a wildly rich city, with lavish palaces hosting visiting royalty and foreign dignitaries. Both public and private wealth left its mark in the old town: Palazzo San Giorgio and the Loggia dei Mercanti on the one hand, the Doria family mansions in Piazza San Matteo and Palazzo Spinola on the other.

The relationship between the old town and the city's nearby port has been a centuries-old problem, with the port all but neglected for decades, but a host of renovations and reopenings over the last 30 years – Renzo Piano's redesigned Porto Antico foremost among them – have redressed the balance. Today, the Centro Storico's sumptuous homes and palaces house museums, cafés and shops, and the area remains the most densely populated historic centre in Europe.

IL CENTRO STORICO

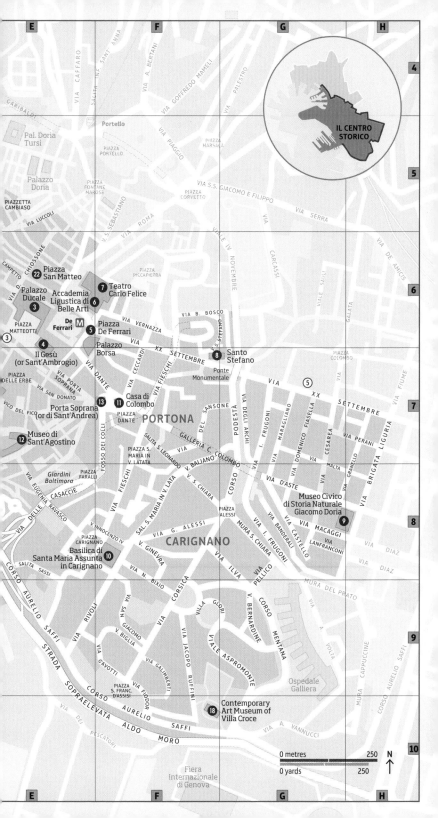

E

GARIBALDI

VIA CAFFARO

VIA SALITA INF. S. ANNA

VIA A. BERTANI

Portello

Pal. Doria
Tursi

PIAZZA
PORTELLO

Palazzo
Doria

PIAZZA
FONTANE
MAROSE

PIAZZETTA
CAMBIASO

VIA LUCCOLI

VIA S. SEBASTIANO

VIA ROMA

F

VIA GOFFREDO MAMELI

VIA PALLESTRO

VIA PIAGGIO

PIAZZA
MARSALA

VIA S.S. GIACOMO E FILIPPO

PIAZZA
CORVETTO

G

4

5

IL CENTRO
STORICO

VIA SERRA

VIA DE AMICIS

H

CAMPETTO

CHIOSSONE

22 Piazza
San Matteo

VIA D. CAMPO

Palazzo
3 Ducale

Accademia
Ligustica di
6 Belle Arti

7 Teatro
Carlo Felice

PIAZZA
PICCAPIETRA

VIA IV NOVEMBRE

CARCASSI

VIALE SAULI

GALATA

6

De
Ferrari **M**

5 Piazza
De Ferrari

VIA VERNAZZA

VIA

VIA B. BOSCO

PIAZZA
MATTEOTTI

3

4
Il Gesù
(or Sant'Ambrogio)

Palazzo
Borsa

VIA CECCARDI

XX SETTEMBRE

VIA FIESCHI

VIA S. STEFANO

8 Santo
Stefano

Ponte
Monumentale

PIAZZA
COLOMBO

VIA FIUME

7

PIAZZA
DELLE ERBE

VIA PORTA
SORANA

VIA SAN DONATO

VICO DEL FICO

VIA DANTE

Porta Soprana
(or di Sant'Andrea)

13 **11** Casa di
Colombo

PIAZZA
DANTE

PORTONA

FOSSO DEL COLLI

VIA DEL SANSONE

GALLERIA C. COLOMBO

VIA DEGLI ARCHI

VIA PODESTÀ

VIA I. FRUGONI

VIA MARIAGLIANO

VIA DOMENICO FIASELLA

5

XX

VIA CESAREA

SETTEMBRE

VIA PERANI

VIA BRIGATA LIGURIA

12 Museo di
Sant'Agostino

SALITA S. LEONARDO

PIAZZA S.
MARIA IN
V. LATATA

V. BALIANO

VIA GRANELLO

VIA MALTA

VIA D'ASTE

7

Giardini
Baltimora

PIAZZA
FARALLI

VIA EUGENIA RAVASCO

CASACCIE

VIA DELLE

VIA INNOCENZO IV

PIAZZA
CARIGNANO

SAL. S. MARIA IN V. LATA

VIA FIESCHI

V. S. CHIARA

CORSO

PIAZZA
ALESSI

VIA G. ALESSI

MURA S. CHIARA

VIA I. FRUGONI

VIA BANDERALI

VIA CASTELLO

VIA MACAGGI

VIA LANFRANCONI

Museo Civico
di Storia Naturale
Giacomo Doria **9**

VIA DIAZ

VIA DIAZ

8

CARIGNANO

Basilica di
Santa Maria Assunta
in Carignano **10**

VIA GINEVRA

VIA N. BIXIO

VIA ILVA

VIA PELLICO

MURA DEL PRATO

SALITA SASSI

CORSO AURELIO SAFFI

STRADA SOPRAELEVATA ALDO MORO

VIA RIVOLI

VIA SAN GIACOMO

V. BIGLIA

VIA GAVOTTI

VIA CORSICA

VILLA GLORI

VIA JACOPO RUFFINI

VIALE ASPROMONTE

V. BERNARDINE

CORSO MENTANA

Ospedale
Galliera

MURA CAPPUCCINE

CORSO AURELIO SAFFI

VIA VOLTA

9

VIA DEI PESCATORI

PIAZZA
S. FRANC.
D'ASSISI

VIA FIODOR

VIA GALIMBERTI

CORSO AURELIO

SAFFI

18 Contemporary
Art Museum of
Villa Croce

VIA A. VANNUCCI

Fiera
Internazionale
di Genova

0 metres   250

0 yards   250

N
↑

10

E   **F**   **G**   **H**

● 🖊 🎥 🛍

SAN LORENZO

📍 E6 🏛 Piazza S Lorenzo Ⓜ De Ferrari ☎ 010 270 0295
🕐 Church: 8am–noon & 3–7pm daily; Museo del Tesoro:
9am–noon & 3–6pm Mon-Sat 🚫 1 May, 25 Dec

A mix of architectural styles, including Romanesque,
Ligurian Gothic and Baroque, San Lorenzo is one of the
city's most intriguing churches. Housed within it, the
Museo del Tesoro chronicles the fortunes of Genoa.

Did You Know?

The walls of San
Lorenzo still house an
unexploded bomb from
World War II.

The church of San Lorenzo (St Lawrence)
was founded in the 9th century and was chosen
as the cathedral because of its secure position
within the city walls. Romanesque-style reconstruction began in the 12th century but was
never completed. The cathedral's present,
primarily Gothic appearance, including the
lower part of the cheerfully striped façade,
dates from the 13th century. Important alterations followed later, however, mainly in the
15th to 17th centuries: these include the rose
window in the upper part of the façade, the
Renaissance cupola by Galeazzo Alessi and
the beautifully frescoed Lercari chapel.

Opened in the 1950s, the Museo del Tesoro
was the work of Caterina Marcenaro and Franco
Albin. Built underground near the chancel, it
is constructed in Promontorio stone, the dark
material typical of medieval Genoa. Objects
brought back during the Republic's forays into
the Holy Land are displayed here. Among the
highlights are the Sacro Catino, a 9th-century
Islamic glass vessel once believed to be the
Holy Grail used by Christ at the Last Supper,
and a 12th-century silver chest believed to
contain the ashes of St John the Baptist, which
is carried in procession through the streets of
Genoa on 24 June.

① The façade
of the 9th-century San
Lorenzo church has a
unique striped aesthetic,
with a lofty bell tower.

② The long nave of
San Lorenzo also has
distinctive black-and-
white striped arches.

③ Intricate lion
sculptures adorn
the steps leading up
to the church doors.

*Two 19th-century
lion sculptures flank
the main steps. A pair
of Romanesque lions
also feature on the
edges of the façade.*

Cappella di San Giovanni
Battista, dedicated to St John
the Baptist, was the work of
Domenico and Elia Gagini
(mid-1400s).

The vault of the presbytery
and the apse bears two
frescoes by painter Lazzaro
Tavarone; in the apse is a
16th century wooden choir.

The rose window was
rebuilt in 1869. The
symbols of the four
Evangelists remain.

The bell tower was
created from the
right-hand tower in
the 16th century.

Romanesque
blind arches

In the right-hand
apse is Crucifix with
Mary, John and
St Sebastian by
Federico Barocci,
painted in 1597.

Black-and-white
striped arches

Marble pillars

Romanesque bas-reliefs
on medieval church doors
illustrate important
doctrinal subjects

↑ Illustration of
San Lorenzo

2

PORTO ANTICO

📍 D6 🅜 De Ferrari ℹ️ www.portoantico.it

Detached from the rest of the city for centuries, the port has been extensively renovated since 1992 and turned into a busy centre. The project was undertaken by renowned architect Renzo Piano, who transformed the district into an attraction in its own right. He did this by restoring disused buildings such as the 19th-century cotton warehouses – now a multiplex cinema and exhibition centre – and by constructing landmarks such as Il Bigo and the Aquarium.

① 🖉

Il Bigo

🏛 Calata Cattaneo 5
🌐 acquariodigenova.it

Inspired by the masts of a ship and designed by Renzo Piano, Il Bigo is a public sculpture offering a revolving panoramic lift. From a height of 40 m (130 ft), this popular attraction offers great views over the port and city.

②

Porta del Molo

🏛 Mura del Molo 16128

Also known as Porta Siberia, this imposing gate was built in 1553 by the Italian architect and urban designer Galeazzo Alessi. Designed as a defensive bulwark for the port, it was also used as a place for the collection of taxes.

③ 🖉

The Biosphere

🏛 Ponte Spinola 16126
🕐 10am-7pm (Nov-Feb: to 5pm; Mar & Oct: to 6pm)
🌐 acquariodigenova.it

Designed by Renzo Piano, the Biosphere was built in 2001. It is a futuristic glasshouse containing all sorts of tropical plants, from mangroves to rubber and cocoa trees, as well as numerous types of ferns, some of which are extremely rare. The Biosphere is home to various species of butterfly and chameleon.

> 💬 INSIDER TIP
> **Boat Trips**
>
> Boat trips from the quays of Porto Antico offer guided tours of Genoa's coast. Hop aboard for lovely panoramas of the city from the sea. Visit *portoantico.it* for a full list of services and companies.

↑ Bustling Porto Antico, with the Biosphere and Il Bigo in the foreground

④ ⟨⟩ ⟨M3⟩ ⟨⟩ ⟨⟩

The Aquarium

📍 Ponte Spinola 16128
🕐 Mar–Jun & Sep: 9am–8pm; Jul & Aug: 8:30am–8pm
🌐 acquariodigenova.it

Another work by Renzo Piano, the Aquarium is the largest of its kind in Europe and attracts more than one million visitors a year. Made with technical help from American architect Peter Chermayeff, the Aquarium is built within a ship anchored in the port. It is one of Genoa's main attractions, with numerous tanks that are viewable from underwater as well as from above. The Aquarium's aim is to help visitors to discover and marvel at different aspects of the sea and to promote understanding of the extent to which human life is linked to the oceans. There are spectacular reconstructions of diverse ecosystems, making it possible to observe animals, habitats and ocean floors at close quarters.

↓ Porto Antico with its many landmarks

EXPERIENCE MORE

3 Palazzo Ducale

📍 E6 🏛 Piazza Matteotti 9
🕐 Palace: 7am-11pm daily;
exhibitions: 10am-7pm
Tue-Sun 🌐 palazzo
ducale.genova.it

Constructed in the Middle Ages, this palazzo was given its name (meaning Doge's Palace) in 1339, when the election of Genoa's first doge, Simone Boccanegra, took place. It was enlarged to its current size in the late 1500s by Andrea Vannone, a Lombard architect. Further major changes were made by Swiss Neo-Classical architect Simone Cantoni following a fire in the late 18th century. These changes included the construction of the façade overlooking Piazza Matteotti (another lively, frescoed façade faces Piazza De Ferrari), which features a series of paired columns and is topped by elaborate statues and trophies.

The palazzo is organized around Vannone's attractive atrium, with a large, elegant, porticoed courtyard at either end. The staircases up to the first floor are lined with frescoes by Lazzaro Tavarone and Domenico Fiasella.

The upper floor has some fine public rooms: the doge's chapel was frescoed by the artist Giovanni Battista Carlone in the 17th century with scenes celebrating the glorious history of the city of Genoa. This theme continues in the decoration of the Sala del Maggior Consiglio and the Sala del Minor Consiglio. The Salone, designed by Simone Cantoni, features paintings by the artist Giovanni David, among many others.

Since the extensive restoration in 1992, the palace has become a venue for major exhibitions. In addition, there are shops, bars and restaurants, including a rooftop restaurant with panoramic views.

___

↑ The lively Piazza De Ferrari, home to the Accademia Ligustica

4 Il Gesù (or Sant'Ambrogio)

📍 E6 🏛 Piazza Matteotti
📞 010 251 4122 🕐 7:45am-
12:50pm & 3:30-7:45pm
Mon-Sat, 7:45am-1pm &
4-10:30pm Sun & public hols

Overlooking Piazza Matteotti, this church was built by the Jesuits. It was begun in 1589, over the existing church of Sant'Ambrogio, and given the name of Il Gesù. The façade, following the original design by Giuseppe Valeriani, was finished only at the end of the 19th century.

The sumptuous Baroque interior consists of a single room topped by a dome. Multi-coloured marble decorates the floor, the pilasters and the walls of the side chapels, and the upper parts of the walls have been finished with gilded stuccoes and frescoes by Giovanni Battista Carlone.

The most valuable paintings in the church all date from the 17th century, including works by Guido Reni and *Crucifixion* by Simon Vouet.

There are also works that were commissioned by the Pallavicino family from Peter Paul Rubens: *Circumcision* and *St Ignatius Exorcising the Devil*, both acknowledged masterpieces and precursors of the typical Baroque style.

↑ Il Gesù's opulent interiors with frescoes on the gilded walls and domed ceilings

⑤ Piazza De Ferrari

📍 E6

This grand piazza, with its large fountain, was built in the late 19th century with the aim of easing the flow of traffic between the Centro Storico and the western side of Genoa. Its design had to accommodate the existing buildings of the Accademia Ligustica di Belle Arti and the Teatro Carlo Felice, both built by Carlo Barabino in the 1820s. The stately palazzi built around these two buildings are eclectic in style.

> 💬 **INSIDER TIP**
> **Genoa Museum Card**
>
> Valid for 24 hours, this card provides access to over 50 museums for a reduced fee, as well as unlimited use of AMT public transport. Visit *museidigenova.it* for more details.

The building of the theatre in 1991, the restoration of the fountain and other alterations, including those of 2001, have given the Piazza De Ferrari a major face-lift.

⑥ Accademia Ligustica di Belle Arti

📍 E6 🏛 **Largo Pertini 4**
🕑 **2:30–6:30pm Tue-Sat**
🌐 **accademialigustica.it**

Founded in 1751 by a group of aristocrats and scholars as a School of Fine Arts, the Accademia occupies a palazzo built for it between 1826–31 by Carlo Barabino. The museum on the first floor displays paintings and drawings donated to the academy. Works of art from the 15th to 19th centuries are arranged chronologically: they include works by major Ligurian artists (Gregorio De Ferrari and Bernardo Strozzi, among others), and artists who were active in Genoa (such as Perin del Vaga and Anton Raphael Mengs).

EAT

Focaccia e Dintorni
Sample some of Genoa's best street food, including delicious focaccia.

📍 D6 🏛 **Via di Canneto Il Curto, 54r**
📞 **010 247 2154**

€€€

Tazze Pazze
A café serving coffee and *sacripantina* cake.

📍 D6 🏛 **Piazza Cinque Lampadi, 71R**
🌐 **tazzepazze.com**

€€€

Caffè degli Specchi
Open since 1908, this café once attracted famous artists.

📍 E6 🏛 **Piazza Unità d'Italia, 7** 📞 **040 661 973**

€€€

Imposing façade of Teatro Carlo Felice, the city's main opera house ↑

Teatro Carlo Felice

♀ F6 ⌂ Passo Eugenio Montale 4 🕑 8:30am-7:30pm Mon-Sat ⚏ opera carlofelicegenova.it

This Neo-Classical theatre was designed in the 1820s by Carlo Barabino. The building was bombed heavily during World War II and only parts of the original façade survived. Reconstruction began in the late 1980s, with the theatre reopening in 1991. Today, it is one of the most advanced theatres in Europe, featuring remarkable acoustics and state-of-the-art technology, including a 63-m- (206-ft-) high stage tower that houses its technical units. The theatre regularly hosts classical music concerts as well as opera and ballet performances. It also offers guided tours.

Legend speaks of the ghost of a 16-year-old girl, Leila Carbone, inhabiting the theatre, which today stands on the site of a medieval convent that was once the seat of the Holy Inquisition. Leila was sentenced for witchcraft but is said to have died of terror before the torture began. The pale, barefoot girl is believed to roam the grounds, which she considers her home.

Santo Stefano

♀ F7 ⌂ Piazza Santo Stefano 2 ☎ 010 587 183 🕑 11:30am-6:30pm Mon, 9:30am-6:30pm Tue-Sat, 9:30am-2pm Sun

Built at the end of the 12th century, the Romanesque church of Santo Stefano stands on the site of a Benedictine abbey. The church underwent major restoration after being damaged in World War II.

The façade features bands of black-and-white striped marble, typical of Pisan and Ligurian Romanesque, with a main door surmounted by an oculus and a mullioned window. The brick-built apse is ornamented by blind arches with arcading above. Its bell tower and 14th-century lantern are also constructed in decorative brick.

Inside, in the presbytery, is *Martyrdom of St Stephen,* a fine work by Giulio Romano, and paintings by various Genoese and Lombard artists, among them Valerio Castello, Gregorio De Ferrari and Giulio Cesare Procaccini.

Museo Civico di Storia Naturale Giacomo Doria

♀ G8 ⌂ Via Brigata Liguria 9 🕑 10am-6:30pm Tue-Sun ⚏ museidigenova.it

Established in 1867 by Marchese Giacomo Doria,

> **Legend speaks of the ghost of a 16-year-old girl, Leila Carbone, inhabiting the Teatro, which today stands on the site of a medieval convent that was once the seat of the Holy Inquisition.**

its director for more than 40 years, Genoa's Natural History Museum contains important zoological finds, many of which were collected in the 19th century. The ground floor has rooms devoted to mammals and reconstructed animal habitats. A definite must-see is the Palaeontology Room, with its skeleton of *Elephus antiquus italicus*, an ancient elephant found near Rome in 1941. On the first floor are displays of reptiles, amphibians, birds, butterflies and insects.

The museum undertakes plenty of educational work and regularly hosts various conferences and exhibitions.

---

⑩

Basilica di Santa Maria Assunta in Carignano

❾F8 **❿Piazza di Carignano** **☎010 540 650** **🕐7:30am-noon & 4:30-7pm Mon-Sat, 8am-12:30pm & 4:30-7:30pm Sun**

This Renaissance church was designed for the hill closest to the centre of the city by Perugian architect Galeazzo Alessi. Construction began in 1549 and took 50 years to complete.

A monumental flight of steps, designed by Alessi but built in the 19th century, leads up to the broad façade, flanked by two elegant bell towers. Rising above is a high central cupola surrounded by four smaller domes.

At the entrance, the elaborate sculptures by Claude David include a statue of the Virgin Mary over the door and statues of saints Peter and Paul in the side niches. A balcony runs along the roofs and around the central dome, making the most of the church's panoramic position.

→

Sculptures adorning the entrance of Basilica di Santa Maria Assunta di Carignano

Inside, the harmonious exterior motif of pilasters with Corinthian capitals continues. As in St Peter's in Rome, the four vast pilasters that support the cupola have niches containing statues: these include *St Sebastian* by Pierre Puget. On the second altar on the right is a *Martyrdom of St Blaise* by Carlo Maratta, and in the sixth on the left a famous *Pietà* by Luca Cambiaso. Other paintings, some of which have been adapted to fit the church's particular setting, are by Domenico Fiasella and Guercino.

---

⑪ Ⓜ

Casa di Colombo

❾F7 **❿Via di Porta Soprana** **🕐10am-6pm Tue-Fri, 10am-7pm Sat & Sun** **🌐museidigenova.it**

Legend has it that this modest house near Porta Soprana was the childhood home of Christopher

Columbus who was born in Genoa in 1451.

The house that visitors can tour today is, in fact, an 18th-century reconstruction: the original was destroyed by cannon fire during a French bombardment in 1684. Restoration was carried out on the building in preparation for the Columbus celebrations of 1992. This work extended to the adjacent 12th-century Chiostro di Sant'Andrea (cloister of St Andrew), all that is left of a Benedictine monastery that was demolished – along with other buildings in the area – at the beginning of the 20th century.

12

Museo di Sant'Agostino

📍E7 🏛Piazza Sarzano 35
🕐9am-6:30pm Tue-Fri,
9:30am-6:30pm Sat & Sun
🌐museidigenova.it

The World War II bombing badly damaged Piazza Sarzano, but this 13th-century monastic church was a lucky survivor. The façade, with its black-and-white stripes, is typically Ligurian, while the elegant bell tower is coated with colourful majolica tiles.

Today, the church serves as an auditorium, and the former Augustinian monastery buildings that are adjacent

---

🔍 HIDDEN GEM
Medieval Walking Tours

Walk through Genoa's medieval streets and discover how the Genoese once navigated the city by mapping out churches and palaces. Check *www.explora tour.it* for details.

– including the two cloisters – have been adapted to house the museum. The collection focuses on sculptures brought here from sites (including demolished churches) all over the city. It also showcases detached frescoes, architectural fragments and examples of Genoese art from the Middle Ages to the 18th century.

13

Porta Soprana (or di Sant'Andrea)

📍F7 🏛Via di Ravecca 47 nero 🏰Towers: closed to public 🌐museidigenova.it

This gate corresponds to an opening made in the walls in the 9th century to connect Genoa to the east. The actual structure, however, was part of a ring of walls built in 1155 to defend Genoa from possible attack by Emperor Frederick I, known as Barbarossa. It is similar to the Porta di Santa Fede, on the other side of the city. Restoration carried out in the 19th and 20th centuries has liberated the historic gate of

the structures added to it over the centuries, and exposed the pointed arch, flanked by a pair of cylindrical battlemented towers that are ornamented by arcading and cornicing.

14

Santa Maria di Castello

📍D7 🏛Salita Santa Maria di Castello 15 🕐Church & Museum: 10am-1pm & 3-6pm daily

Rising on the site of the Roman *castrum*, or fort (around which the earliest parts of the city were constructed), this 12th-century church is among the most illustrious of old Genoese churches. It was built on the site of an earlier place of worship, at a time when Romanesque buildings were appearing all over the city.

In the mid-15th century, the church was entrusted to the Dominicans, who added monastic buildings, including three cloisters. The latters' decoration was commissioned by the Grimaldi family, who, through private patronage,

The towers of the 12th-century Porta Soprana

←

Interior of the San Donato church with its stone pillars and wooden roof

On the right-hand side of the church is a shrine with a statue of the *Madonna and Child*. It is one of many erected in the Centro Storico. The charming interior has a nave and two aisles, with Corinthian columns and a gallery of windows above – some of the columns are Roman.

A *Madonna and Child* by Nicolò da Voltri is on the altar in the right-hand apse and, in the chapel of San Giuseppe in the left-hand aisle, there is a panelled triptych by the Flemish painter Joos van Cleve that depicts an *Adoration of the Magi* in the central panel.

turned the complex into a point of reference for local artists. Over time, other aristocratic families commissioned the decoration of the church's side chapels.

The stone façade is crowned by a cornice of blind arches. Its central doorway incorporates a Roman architrave, and there are other Roman elements inside: several of the Corinthian capitals that adorn the red granite columns in the nave came from Roman buildings, and in the Cappella del Battistero is a sarcophagus of Roman origin.

The apse, the chapels and the dome are the result of changes made from the 15th to the 18th centuries. In the chapel's left transept is a *Virgin with the saints Catherine and Mary Magdalen and the effigies of St Dominic* by Giovanni Benedetto Castiglione. In the high altar is a late 17th-century marble sculpture of the *Assumption*.

Among the monastic buildings, the second cloister is of special note. Here, the Loggia dell'Annunciazione, features roundels with *Sibyls* and *Prophets* in its vault, and a charming fresco of the *Annunciation* by Justus von Ravensburg.

There is a small museum, with works such as *Paradise* and *The Conversion of St Paul* by Ludovico Brea; an *Immaculate Conception*, a wooden sculpture by Maragliano; and a *Madonna and Child* by Barnaba da Modena.

Next to the church stands the 12th-century Torre degli Embriaci, evidence of the medieval power of the aristocratic Embriaci family, who lived in this quarter.

15

San Donato

9 E7 **1** Via San Donato 10 **C** 010 246 8869 **9** 10am-noon & 3:30-6:30pm Mon-Sat, Sun 10am-noon

This 12th-century Romanesque church features a splendid octagonal bell tower erected over the church crossing. Its three levels (the third is a 19th-century addition) are each pierced by windows. The tower was chosen as a model by the designers of the north tower of San Benigno, the so-called "Matitone" (great pencil) in the Porto Antico (*p62*).

Its façade carries noticeable features from the late 19th-century alterations, when the rose window was added. The main doorway is original and of particular beauty: it incorporates a Roman architrave in the moulding.

DRINK

Rebus

This cocktail bar is great for an aperitivo. Soak up panoramic port views from its terrace.

9 C4 **1** Calata Salumi, 16126 **C** 010 091 0148

MOG Mercato Orientale

Enjoy a glass or two of local vino at one of the many bars and restaurants in this market.

9 G7 **1** Via XX Settembre, 75 **W** moggenova.it

Ai Troëggi

Pair artisanal beers and natural wines with bruschettas, which are prepared with all sorts of tasty toppings.

9 D6 **1** Via Chiabrera, 61 **C** 349 719 7363

16
Loggia dei Mercanti

**📍 D5 🏠 Piazza Banchi
Ⓜ San Giorgio**

This Renaissance loggia was built to a design by Andrea Vannone, in order to accommodate the work of the city's money changers. The loggia was a typical element of buildings intended for commerce during the Middle Ages.

The loggia in Piazza Banchi is built on a rectangular plan and has a single barrel vault supported by arches resting on paired columns – its openings were glassed in during the 19th century. The exterior features a sculptured frieze by Taddeo Carlone, and the interior has a fresco of the

Did You Know?

In 1855, the Loggia dei Mercanti became the seat of Italy's first trade Stock Exchange.

Madonna and Child and saints John the Baptist and George by Pietro Sorri. The building now hosts occasional exhibitions.

17
Palazzo San Giorgio

📍 D6 🏠 Via della Mercanzia 2 Ⓜ San Giorgio

The Palazzo San Giorgio is traditionally identified as the place in which Marco Polo was imprisoned following the Battle of Curzola in 1298. While he was here, Polo met a writer from Pisa called Rustichello, with whom he joined forces after their release to write *Il Milione (The Travels)*.

The palazzo is made up of two distinct parts: a medieval part facing the city, which was built in 1260 as the seat of the government (the Capitani del Popolo), and later became the Banco di San Giorgio in 1407; and a second part, a huge 16th-century extension built to overlook the port. The fresco decoration by Lazzaro Tavarone on the latter's façade was discovered

only during restoration work in the 1990s.

The expansion of the palazzo, which involved major restructuring of the medieval section, was required because of the rise in power of the Banco di San Giorgio. The bank administered the proceeds from taxes collected by the Republic and also ran the Republic's colonies. It was responsible for much of Genoa's prosperity in the 15th century. Today, the palace houses the offices of the harbour authorities.

Inside, the Salone delle Compere is decorated with 16th-century statues of the Protettori del Banco (protectors of the bank) and the *Arms of Genoa with the symbols of Justice and Strength* by Francesco De Ferrar.

The Sala dei Protettori features a monumental hearth by Italian sculptor Giovanni Giacomo della Porta. Visitors can also see the Sala del Capitano del Popolo, and the Manica Lunga, a 128-m- (420-ft-) long corridor which once served as a vast dormitory for resident Benedictine monks.

← Boats moored at the scenic Old Port, where *(inset)* the frescoed façade of the Palazzo San Giorgio lies

and abstract art from 1930 to 1980 (including work by Fontana and Licini). The museum also holds works by regional artists and promotes young talent by organizing exhibitions and assembling a digital archive of material related to local arts.

GREAT VIEW
City Watching

The Contemporary Art Museum is situated on the hill of Carignano. From outside, there are views over the centre of the city and out across the sea beyond.

---

18 (icons)

Contemporary Art Museum of Villa Croce

📍 F10 🏛 Jacopo Ruffini 3 Ⓜ San Giorgio ⏰ Villa: 11am–6pm Tue–Fri, noon–7pm Sat & Sun 🌐 museidigenova.it

The Museo d'Arte Contemporanea, in the residential district of Carignano, south of the city centre, is surrounded by a large park overlooking the sea. It occupies a late 19th-century Classical-style villa, which was donated to the city by the Croce family in 1951. The museum currently possesses some 3,000 works, which document, in particular, Italian graphic arts

crossroads of major lines of communication between the city and the port. By the Middle Ages there was already a thriving grain market in the piazza, and money changers also set up their stalls here, attracting merchants from all over the world – the piazza is named after the money changers' tables. Later, money changers and other traders worked in the 16th-century Loggia dei Mercanti.

Nearby is the 12th-century arcaded street, Via Sottoripa, which was designed so that its merchants could benefit from the accessibility of the port. Today, the street is home to shops selling various local foods, and there are bars, too.

Founded in the 9th century, the church of **San Pietro in Banchi** was destroyed by a fire that damaged the square in 1398, but rebuilding work did not begin until the 16th century. The project involved raising the church on a terrace, allowing for the construction of shops on the ground level. The church itself is reached by means of a scenic flight of steps that lead to a frescoed façade by the artist Giovanni Battista Baiardo, which was carefully restored in the 1990s. Inside is a marble high altar mensa and an 18th-century crucifix. On top of the altar is an octagonal dome with three pinnacles featuring elaborate sculptures.

19 Piazza Banchi

📍 D6 Ⓜ San Giorgio

Set near the harbour, Piazza Banchi was the commercial core of the city up until the 18th century, and a crucial

↑ One of the many restaurants along the Via Sottoripa next to Piazza Banchi

⑳ Santa Maria delle Vigne

⊙ E5 ⌂ Vico Campanile delle Vigne ⊙ 8am-7pm daily ⊡ chiesadigenova.it

This 11th-century church was founded in an area once planted with vines *(vigne)*. Its Romanesque bell tower is the only original element to have survived. Around 1640, the church was completely rebuilt in Baroque style, and more changes have been made since. The façade (1842) is by architect Ippolito Cremona.

Inside, a nave and two aisles are bathed in sumptuous gilding, stucco and fresco decoration, dating from different periods. The presbytery was frescoed in 1612 by Lazzaro Tavarone, with a *Glory of Mary*, and the aisles and the octagonal cupola were painted by various artists from the 18th to the early 20th century. The church contains paintings by Gregorio De Ferrari, Bernardo Castello and Domenico Piola, and a tablet depicting a Madonna, attributed to Taddeo di Bartolo.

㉑ Palazzo Spinola di Pellicceria

⊙ D5 ⌂ Piazza Pellicceria 1 Ⓜ San Giorgio ☎ 010 270 5343 ⊙ 9am-7pm Wed-Sat, 1:30-7pm first Sun only ⊡ palazzospinola. beniculturali.it

With all the elegance of an old aristocratic mansion house, this palazzo is richly frescoed and has luxurious furnishings and paintings. Built in the 16th century by the Grimaldi family, the palazzo passed to the Spinola family in the 18th century, and they eventually donated it to the state in 1958.

The first two floors house the Galleria Nazionale di Palazzo Spinola. The rooms have been restored to their original style, with paintings arranged as if this were still a private home. Two fresco cycles illustrate the main phases in the history of the palazzo: one, by Lazzaro Tavarone, illustrates

---

CENTRO STORICO'S DOORWAY SCULPTURES

Sculpted from marble or the black stone of Promontorio, Genoa's door carvings emerged due to economic constraints and a shortage of space. In the 15th century, noble families expanded the ground floors of their palazzi to accommodate shops, resulting in elaborate doorways like those of Palazzo Spinola. Famous sculptors (particularly members of the Gagini family) developed this unique craft.

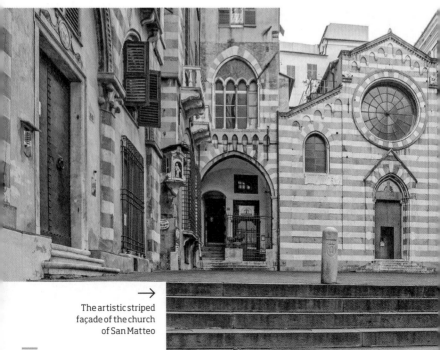

→ The artistic striped façade of the church of San Matteo

in two rooms *Exploits and Personalities in the Grimaldi family*, while the other decorates the Galleria degli Specchi (Hall of Mirrors) and salons, the work of Lorenzo De Ferrari for the Spinola family. The Spinola donation includes works by Guido Reni, Giovanni Benedetto Castigliona and van Dyck.

On the third floor, the Galleria Nazionale della Liguria is reserved for works that were not part of the Spinola donation, including fine artworks such as *Ecce Homo* by Antonello da Messina, *an Equestrian Portrait of Gio Carlo Doria* by Rubens and *Justice*, sculpted by Giovanni Pisano.

---

22 ✎

Piazza San Matteo

📍 E6 🏛 Chiesa di San Matteo Ⓜ De Ferrari
☎ 010 2474361

From the 12th to the 17th centuries, this lovely

square was the headquarters of the powerful Doria family, which, in common with the other powerful Genoese dynasties, gathered its political clique in a distinct area of the city. Despite changes to the palazzi facing the square, the piazza has kept its original compact form and a distinct charm – something that is missing from other similar areas.

The buildings bear typical wall coverings of striped black-and-white marble, characteristic of Gothic civic buildings. Of particular note is Palazzo di Lamba Doria, at no. 15, named after the family member who defeated the Venetian fleet at Curzola in 1298 – the typical structure of a medieval Genoese palazzo is still in evidence. Also noteworthy is Palazzo di Doria Quartara Doria, at no. 14.

The small church of San Matteo, the family place of worship of the Dorias, was built in 1125, and then

rebuilt in the late 13th century in Gothic style. Pilasters divide the black-and-white striped façade into three, corresponding to the aisles. The interior was altered in the 16th century for Andrea Doria, who is buried in the crypt, as is his ancestor Lamba Doria. Giovanni Battista Castello, in collaboration with the artist Luca Cambiaso, modified the nave and aisles and painted the nave vault. The statues in the apse niches and the decoration of the presbytery and the cupola are by Angelo Montorsoli.

To the left of the church is a pretty cloister, with pointed arches resting on slim paired columns.

A SHORT WALK

AROUND PIAZZA MATTEOTTI

Distance 1 km (0.5 miles) **Time** 10 minutes
Nearest metro Sarzano

The dense warren of the Centro Storico has numerous open squares among its alleys, including Piazza San Lorenzo and Piazza Matteotti, the latter in front of the Palazzo Ducale. Nearby is Piazza De Ferrari, a 19th-century project, which links the old city with the modern and industrial part of Genoa. There are numerous monuments of interest in this area: churches of ancient origin such as Santa Maria di Castello, Santa Maria delle Vigne and Sant'Agostino, as well as public and private buildings, including the supposed birthplace of Christopher Columbus, the Palazzo Spinola di Pellicceria, and Palazzo San Giorgio, from whose frescoed façade there are beautiful views of the sea. Take your time strolling the area, enjoying the views of striking palazzi from one of the piazzas.

Did You Know?

The piazza is named after politician Giacomo Matteotti, murdered in 1924 for opposing Mussolini.

Palazzo Spinola

PIAZZA CAMPETT

VIA DI SCURRERIA

VIA ARCIV

The cathedral of **San Lorenzo** *(p60) was surrounded by the medieval city until the building of Via San Lorenzo alongside the church in the mid-19th century.*

START

VIA SAN LORENZO

The port, Piazza Banchi and Palazzo San Giorgio

Museo di Sant'Agostino
(p68), set in the ruined church of Sant'Agostino, houses relics from around the city, including the 17th-century Madonna and Child by Pierre Puget.

VICO TRE RE MAGI

FINISH

← Busy Via San Lorenzo leading to San Lorenzo from Piazza Matteotti

↑ Studying the architecture of Palazzo Ducale's courtyard

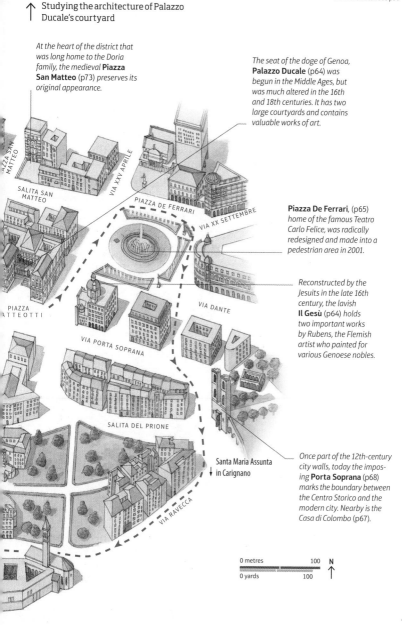

At the heart of the district that was long home to the Doria family, the medieval **Piazza San Matteo** (p73) preserves its original appearance.

The seat of the doge of Genoa, **Palazzo Ducale** (p64) was begun in the Middle Ages, but was much altered in the 16th and 18th centuries. It has two large courtyards and contains valuable works of art.

Piazza De Ferrari, (p65) home of the famous Teatro Carlo Felice, was radically redesigned and made into a pedestrian area in 2001.

Reconstructed by the Jesuits in the late 16th century, the lavish **Il Gesù** (p64) holds two important works by Rubens, the Flemish artist who painted for various Genoese nobles.

Once part of the 12th-century city walls, today the imposing **Porta Soprana** (p68) marks the boundary between the Centro Storico and the modern city. Nearby is the Casa di Colombo (p67).

Santa Maria Assunta
↓ in Carignano

0 metres   100   N
0 yards   100   ↑

LE STRADE NUOVE

The district known as Le Strade Nuove (or "new streets") has its origins in the 16th and 17th centuries, the pinnacle of Genoa's financial power. The so-called "Genoese Century" lasted from 1528 to 1630, when the power of the city's noble families was at its height and Genoa was a dominant force in European finance. The city's wealthiest families poured their money into new buildings and extravagant art commissions, setting their new palaces aside from the medieval centre of the Centro Storico. The complexity of these Renaissance designs, coupled with the city's uneven terrain, made for palazzi of lavish beauty and architectural extravagance. The artist Peter Paul Rubens held the palazzi on Via Garibaldi, with their loggias and hanging gardens, in such high esteem that he made detailed drawings and published an influential architectural study.

Le Strade Nuove and the assortment of Renaissance and Baroque palaces known as the Palazzi dei Rolli now collectively comprise a UNESCO World Heritage site. Many of the palaces are open to the public, with Palazzo Rosso, Palazzo Bianco and Palazzo Doria Tursi on Via Garibaldi jointly constituting the Strada Nuova Museums.

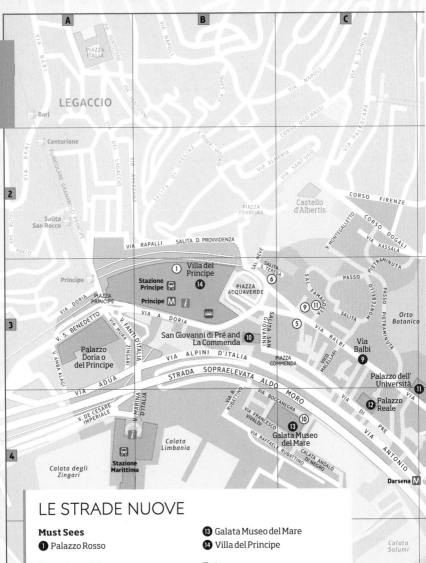

LE STRADE NUOVE

Must Sees
1 Palazzo Rosso

Experience More
2 Palazzo Blanco
3 Piazza Fontane Marose
4 Museo di Arte Orientale Edoardo Chiossone
5 Palazzo Doria Tursi
6 San Siro
7 Santissima Annunziata del Vastato
8 Albergo dei Poveri
9 Via Balbi
10 San Giovanni di Pré and La Commenda
11 Palazzo dell'Università
12 Palazzo Reale
13 Galata Museo del Mare
14 Villa del Principe

Eat
1 Profumo di Rosa
2 Gelateria Profumo
3 Cremeria Buonefede

Stay
4 Hotel de Ville
5 Ostello Bello Genova
6 Grand Hotel Savoia
7 Hotel Cairoli

Shop
8 Camomilla Italia
9 Gelateria Balbi
10 Salumeria
11 HB Gourmet Gastronomia

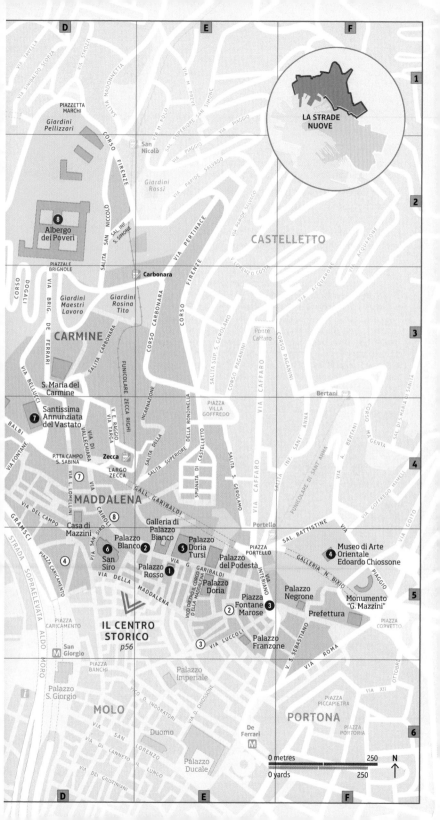

EXPERIENCE **Le Strade Nuove**

① ⊗ 🏛

PALAZZO ROSSO

📍E5 🏠 Via Garibaldi 18 🕐 Apr-Oct: 9am-7pm Tue-Fri,
10am-7:30pm Sat & Sun; Nov-Mar: 9am-6:30pm Tue-Fri,
9:30am-6:30pm Sat & Sun 🌐 museidigenova.it

One of the most striking buildings on the Via Garibaldi,
this sumptuous museum – along with the Palazzo
Doria-Tursi and Palazzo Bianco *(p82)* – forms the Musei
di Strada Nuova. Its world-class art collection features
some true highlights of European painting.

Palazzo Rosso, which owes its name to its reddish exterior,
is an opulent mansion on Via Garibaldi. It was built for the
noble, ultra-wealthy Brignole-Sale family in the 1670s. The
palazzo's art collection was spearheaded by brothers Gio
Francesco and Ridolfo Maria Brignole-Sale, and it grew under
the family until the Duchess di Galliera, Maria Brignole-Sale De
Ferrari, bequeathed the palace and the collection to the city in
1874. Palazzo Rosso was damaged during World War II, but
architect Franco Albini's restoration in the 1950s recaptured
the majesty of the original building. Inside, the frescoes, gilt
and stuccowork are as much to be admired as the art.

Did You Know?

The Palazzo's
magnificent ceiling
fresco by Gregorio De
Ferrari was destroyed
in World War II.

→

The decadent interiors of
Palazzo Rosso, a unique
house-turned-museum

←
The museum's iconic red exterior, as seen from the garden facing it

GALLERY GUIDE

The main artworks are distributed between 33 rooms on the two main floors (an additional 19 rooms are on the mezzanine and third floor). On the first floor are works by Guido Reni and Guercino, as well as works by Genoese artists such as Bernardo Strozzi. On the second floor, the magnificently decorated rooms are a big attraction, particularly the Sale delle Stagioni, along with the portraits of Brignole-Sale by Anthony Van Dyck. The gallery also has the finest library of art history in Liguria, as well as an education centre that organizes activities for children.

Gallery Highlights

Allegory of Spring by Gregorio De Ferrari

▶ When Gregorio De Ferrari painted this allegory (1686-7) in the Sale delle Stagioni, he used the scene in which Venus seduces Mars. This masterpiece of Baroque "illusionism" was the fruit of the collaboration between De Ferrari and artists skilled in perspective and stucco-work. Other seasonal allegories, painted by Domenico Piola, are in Rooms 19–22 of the palazzo.

Portraits by Van Dyck

▶ Portraits of the Brignole-Sale family by the Flemish artist Van Dyck in Room 29 include those of Anton Giulio, Geronima and Paolina. Painted while he was a resident in Genoa, they are stunning examples of his later work. Giulio's portrait is particularly notable, showing the 22-year-old frozen in a pose otherwise reserved for sovereigns - a superb affirmation of his social status. The halls of the Palazzo Rosso also house masterpieces of Van Dyck's early career.

Portrait of a Young Man by Albrecht Dürer

▶ This work, dated 1506, can be found in Room 13. It was produced during Dürer's second trip to Italy. In abandoning the traditional sideways profile, the subject is brought into more direct contact with the onlooker. The painting was subject to excessively vigorous cleaning in the 20th century, which has caused some damage. It remains, however, a great example of Dürer's work while he was in Italy.

Alcova

▶ This enchanting 18th-century room is decorated with impressive frescoes enclosed by lavish amounts of gilt and stuccowork. It is furnished with a large, ornate bridal bed (c 1780) and features stunning pastel portraits of the Brignole-Sale family. These private rooms underwent extensive renovation before they were reopened to the public in 2022.

Must See

↑ The graceful exterior of Palazzo Bianco

EXPERIENCE MORE

②

Palazzo Bianco

**⊙ E5 ⌂ Via Garibaldi 18
⌨ ⊙ 9am–7pm Tue–Fri,
10am–7:30pm Sat & Sun
(Nov–Mar: to 6:30pm)
ⓦ museidigenova.it**

Palazzo Bianco, located at the end of Via Garibaldi, was built in the mid-16th century for the Grimaldi family. It was altered in 1714 for Maria Durazzo Brignole-Sale, who introduced a new white façade, perhaps to distinguish it from the nearby Palazzo Rosso, the first home of the Brignole family.

In 1888, the palazzo and its art collection, including collections assembled by its later occupants, were donated to Genoa by Maria de Ferrari, Duchess of Galliera, the last descendant of the Brignole family (who also donated the Palazzo Rosso to the city).

The gallery offers a tour of Genoese painting, as well as many great European paintings from the 13th to the 18th centuries. Genoese artists represented include Luca Cambiaso, Bernardo Strozzi and Alessandro Magnasco, whose famous *Trattenimento in un Giardino di Albaro* is on display here. There is also an important core of Flemish paintings, with works by Gerard David, van Dyck and Rubens, as well as paintings by Murillo, Filippino Lippi, Caravaggio and Veronese.

---

③

Piazza Fontane Marose

⊙ E5 ⌨

This square owes its name to an ancient *fonte* (fountain), which was recorded in a 13th-century document but destroyed in the 19th century. The attractive piazza is free of traffic, but has an "assembled" look, the result of numerous changes in the layout and of the variations in street levels.

Among the palazzi facing onto the square, the main one, at no. 6, is Palazzo Spinola "dei Marmi", built in the mid-15th century and so-called because of its typically elegant covering of black-and-white striped *marmo* (marble). The palazzo's design had to adapt to the extremely uneven terrain and pre-dates the building of the palazzi in Via Garibaldi.

The only building in the piazza contemporaneous with the buildings on Via Garibaldi is Palazzo Interiano Pallavicini (no. 2), which was constructed in 1565 by Francesco Casella.

---

④

Museo di Arte Orientale Edoardo Chiossone

**⊙ F5 ⌂ Villetta Di Negro,
Piazzale Mazzini 4 ⌨
⊙ 9am–7pm Tue–Fri,
10am–7:30pm Sat & Sun
ⓦ museidigenova.it**

Genoa's Museum of Oriental Art is set within the Parco della Villetta Di Negro, which was designed as a garden of acclimatization for exotic plants by the nobleman Ippolito Durazzo at the beginning of the 19th century. The gardens are still planted with the original mix of Mediterranean and rare plants. Towards the top of the park is a villa, which houses the museum.

What is one of Europe's foremost collections of east Asian art is named after Genoese painter and engraver, Edoardo Chiossone, who, from 1875 to 1898, ran the Printing Bureau of the Ministry of Finance in Tokyo, designing banknotes for the Japanese government. He also became a respected portrait painter at the Japanese court, as well as an avid art collector. Chiossone bequeathed his collection of around 15,000 pieces to Genoa's Accademia Ligustica, where he had trained. These pieces, some of which are exceedingly rare, include paintings, prints, lacquerware, enamels, sculptures, ceramics, textiles and an exceptional collection of Samurai armour.

5 ⬡

Palazzo Doria-Tursi

📍 E5 🏛 Via Garibaldi 18 🚌 ⏰ 9am-7pm Tue-Fri, 10am-7:30pm Sat & Sun (Nov-Mar: to 6:30pm) 🌐 museidigenova.it

Constructed for Nicolò Grimaldi (so rich that he was nicknamed "monarca" by his fellow citizens), this enormous palazzo breaks the previously maintained

→ Grand façade of Palazzo Doria-Tursi, Genoa's town hall

coherence of Via Garibaldi, and stands out in striking contrast. Constructed in 1569–79 by Domenico and Giovanni Ponzello, with the help of sculptor Taddeo Carlone, the palazzo was acquired in 1596 by the Doria family, and remained in their possession until 1848, when it was bought by Emperor Vittorio Emanuele I and became the seat of the town council.

Its distinctive exterior incorporates the varied colours of the stone: a mixture of white marble, local pink Finale stone and slate tiles. A high plinth unites the central section with two airy side loggias. The latter were built in the late 16th century for the Doria but they blend in so neatly with the whole façade that they look like they were part of the original design.

Inside is one of the most magnificent courtyards in Genoa, with a grand staircase that splits elegantly into two after the first flight. The clock tower was added in 1820. Despite the uneven ground, the rooms flow harmoniously through the palazzo. There is an excellent museum showcasing decorative and applied arts, coins and ceramics. Highlights of the collection include a 1742 violin owned by Niccolò Paganini and various manuscripts relating to Christopher Columbus, including three signed letters.

SHOP

Camomilla Italia

This popular local store sells quality clothing from esteemed Italian fashion brands, often at discounted prices.

📍 B3 🏛 Piazza Acquaverde 16126 🌐 camomillaitalia.com

Gelateria Balbi

Featuring a charming interior and run by friendly staff, this historic ice cream shop sells all manner of sweet, frozen delights.

📍 C3 🏛 Via Balbi 165 ☎ 010 585 40118

Salumeria

This charming family-run delicatessen sells the finest cured meats and local cheeses, along with Liguria's much-loved pesto.

📍 C4 🏛 Via Galata 41 ☎ 010 2465 529

HB Gourmet Gastronomia

This popular deli offers delicious Genoese staples including pesto, foccaccia and pizza.

📍 C3 🏛 1 Via Balbi 27 ☎ 010 261 950

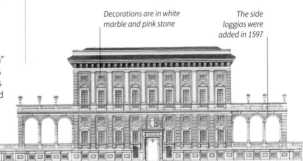

Decorations are in white marble and pink stone

The side loggias were added in 1597

> Following a fire in 1478, San Siro was reconstructed under the supervision of the Theatines, an order of Italian monks established to oppose the Reformation.

6

San Siro

🄯 D5 ⌂ Via San Siro 3
🕐 7:30am–noon & 4–7pm Mon–Sat, 9:30am–12:30pm & 5–6:30pm Sun

A church of ancient foundation, San Siro was Genoa's cathedral until the 9th century, when that title passed to the larger San Lorenzo.

Following a fire in 1478, San Siro was reconstructed under the supervision of the Theatines, an order of Italian monks established to oppose the Reformation by raising the tone of piety in the Roman Catholic church. The church's current appearance dates from this period, though the façade was the later work of architect Carlo Barabino (1821).

Inside, there are three broad aisles with frescoes and stuccoes by Giovanni Battista and Tommaso Carlone, respectively (second half of the 17th century). In the presbytery, adorned with multicoloured marbles, is a monumental high altar in bronze and black marble, a fine work by Pierre Puget (1670). Also of interest in the church is *Annunciation* by Orazio Gentileschi (1639).

Several side chapels were decorated by Domenico Fiasella, Domenico Piola and Gregorio De Ferrari, who also painted the canvases in the church sacristy.

7

Santissima Annunziata del Vastato

🄯 D4 ⌂ Piazza della Nunziata 4 🕐 7:30am–8pm Mon–Fri & Sun, 7:30 am–noon & 2–8pm Sat ⏹ During services

The name of this church combines the two names, one past and one present, of the square that it looks onto. Now Piazza della Nunziata, the square was originally Piazza del Vastato, a name derived from *guastum* or *vastinium*. These terms referred to the fact that the district, which was not enclosed within the city walls, was free from the restrictions that could prevent its use by the military.

The original church dates from 1520, but it was rebuilt in the 16th and 17th centuries for the powerful Lomellini family. Its location was chosen at the intersection of two streams, both of which were channelled into underground waterways in the 17th century; the water was used by the wool industry that was found nearby. The church's façade has two bell towers, with a large 19th-century pronaos (or portico).

The rich interior decoration is thought to be the work of the brothers Giovanni and

←

Façade of San Siro church, designed by architect Barabino

← The richly decorated interior of Santissima Annunziata del Vastato

Giovan Battista Carlone in 1627–8, involving other important artists such as Gioacchino Assereto, Giovanni Andrea Ansaldo and Giulio Benso over the ensuing decades. The central nave is dedicated to glorifying the divinity of Christ and of the Virgin Mary. In the vaults of the transepts, frescoes by Giovanni Carlone depict the *Ascension* and *Pentecost*. The *Assumption of Mary* in the cupola was painted by Andrea Ansaldo and later restored by Gregorio De Ferrari.

GREAT VIEW
Castelletto at Sunset

An Art Nouveau lift heads to the neighbourhood of Castelletto, where you can soak up views of the city. It's a great way of skipping the steep hills near the Albergo dei Poveri.

In the side aisles are frescoed scenes from the Old and New Testaments. The frescoes in the presbytery and the apse (*Annunciation* and *Assumption*), by Giulio Benso, are placed within a grandiose painted architectural framework.

8
Albergo dei Poveri

📍 D2 🏛 Piazzale Brignole 2
🕐 8am-7pm Mon-Fri

The grand white façade of the vast Albergo dei Poveri, with the Genoa city coat of arms at the centre, looms above the Via Brignole De Ferrari. One of Italy's earliest charitable institutions, providing food, lodging and medical care for the poor and the sick, it was established in the 1600s under the patronage of Emanuele Brignole.

The former poorhouse is laid out around four courtyards, with a church at the centre. In more than 300 years of existence, Albergo dei Poveri has housed several artworks, sculptures and pictorial works from different European and Italian schools. Works of art housed here include paintings by the late Renaissance painter Giovanni Battista Paggi, the French painter and sculptor Pierre Puget and the Genoese painter Domenico Piola. The building is now owned by the University of Genoa, and some rooms are used for classes and lectures.

Nearby are the Salita di San Bartolomeo del Carmine and the Salita San Nicolò, perfectly preserved narrow uphill streets (*creuze*) that were once on the city's outskirts but have now been absorbed into the city centre. Genoa's *creuze* were designed to link the sea to the upper streets; lifts also operate throughout the city.

↑ The cobbled Via Balbi, lined with colourful houses, leading to the centre of town

⑨ Via Balbi

⑨ C3

This street, leading from Piazza della Nunziata, was one of the original Strade Nuove. Created in 1602 by Bartolomeo Bianco for the powerful Balbi family, its building was the result of a deal between the Balbi and the government, which ostensibly aimed to improve traffic flow in the area. Ironically, Via Balbi can occasionally be clogged with traffic, though efforts have been made to rectify this. By 1620, seven palazzi had been built, creating the Balbis' very own residential quarter. Sadly, none of the palazzi are open to the public.

At no. 1, Palazzo Durazzo Pallavicini, one of the many residences to have been designed by Bianco, has a lovely atrium and a superb 18th-century staircase. Palazzo Balbi Senarega, another Bianco work at no. 4, is now a university faculty. Inside are fine frescoes by Gregorio De Ferrari.

⑩ San Giovanni di Pré and La Commenda

⑨ B3 ⑥ Piazza della Commenda 1 Ⓜ Principe ⓒ 010 265 486 ⓞ Upper church: 9am–noon & 4–7pm Mon–Wed & Fri, 9am–noon Thu & Sun; lower church: 10am–6pm Fri–Sat; Museum La Commenda: 10am–5pm Tue–Fri (Sat & Sun: to 7pm)

A stone's throw from the main railway station, the church of San Giovanni di Pré was founded in 1180 by the Knights of the Order of St John. The original Romanesque church was largely rebuilt in the 14th century. The bell tower was left untouched.

The main church consists of two churches, one above the other. The lower one, which was always intended for public worship, has three aisles with cross vaults. The upper church was used by the Knights of the Order and was opened to the public only in the 18th century. The upper church is similar in style to the lower church, though it is larger. Heavy columns support Gothic arches between the aisles and ribbed vaults. There are paintings by Giulio Benso, Bernardo Castello and Lazzaro Tavarone. La Commenda, next door, was founded by the Knights of St John in the 11th century to provide lodgings for pilgrims waiting to sail to the Holy Land. It also functioned as a hospital.

Its portico, topped by two loggias, faces onto Piazza della Commenda. There are wonderful frescoes on the third floor. The complex was rebuilt in the 16th century, but restoration work in the 1970s revived its Romanesque appearance. Exhibitions and cultural events are held here.

A short walk eastwards, along Via di Pré (derived from "prati", meaning fields, a reminder of how rural this area once was), leads to the Porta dei Vacca (or Santa Fede), a Gothic arch much altered by the addition of subsequent buildings.

→ The ornate garden terrace of Palazzo Reale

⑪

Palazzo dell'Università

📍D4 🏛️Via Balbi 5
Ⓜ️Principe ☎️010 209 91
🕐7am-7pm Mon-Fri, 7am-noon Sat

Perhaps the most famous building on Via Balbi, this palazzo was built as a Jesuit college in 1634–6 to a design by Bartolomeo Bianco. It has functioned as the seat of the University of Genoa since 1775. Today it houses the rectorate and several faculties. In the Great Hall (Aula Magna), there is a series of six statues by Giambologna personifying the theological and cardinal virtues.

The Biblioteca Universitaria (university library), occupies the adjacent former church of saints Gerolamo and Francesco Saverio. The apse, with some fine frescoes by Domenico Piola, has been transformed into a reading room.

---

⑫

Palazzo Reale

📍C4 🏛️Via Balbi 10 🚏
🕐9am-7pm Wed-Sat, 1:30-7pm Tue & first Sun of the month 🌐palazzoreale genova.cultura.gov.it

Constructed for the Balbi family in 1643–55, this fine palazzo was rebuilt for Eugenio Durazzo only 50 years later. Its new designer, Carlo Fontana, opted for a Baroque mansion, modelled on a Roman palazzo. The building acquired its present name in 1825, when it became the Genoa residence of the royal House of Savoy. Fontana's internal courtyard is striking, and offers fine views over the port. The superb mosaic pavement in the garden came from a monastery.

The palazzo's magnificent rooms, decorated in the 18th and 19th centuries by the Durazzo family and by the Savoys, now form part of the Galleria Nazionale.

The 18th-century rooms include the lavish Galleria degli Specchi (Hall of Mirrors), with a ceiling frescoed by Domenico Parodi. Rooms created by the Savoys include the Sala del Trono (Throne Room), Sala delle Udienze (Audience Chamber) and the Salone da Ballo (Ballroom). The most valuable works of art in the museum include sculptures by Francesco Schiaffino and Filippo Parodi and paintings by Luca Giordano, Van Dyck, Bernardo Strozzi and Valerio Castello.

EAT

Profumo di Rosa

Head to this artisanal ice cream parlour for a refreshing gelato to enjoy on your evening *passeggiata*.

D4 **Via Cairoli 13** **347 092 6454**

€€€

Gelateria Profumo

At this award-winning gelateria, ice creams are lovingly prepared using top-quality ingredients, such as hazelnuts and seasonal fruits.

E4 **Vico Superiore del Ferro 14** **010 251 4159**

€€€

Cremeria Buonafede

This historic spot is the best place to try the city's much-loved *panera genovese*, light and fluffy whipped cream with coffee.

E4 **Via Luccoli** **cremeriabuonafede.it**

€€€

13

Galata Museo del Mare

C4 **Calata De Mari 1** **Darsena** **Nov-Feb: 10am-6pm Tue-Sun (Sat & Sun: to 7:30pm); Mar-Oct: 10am-7:30pm Tue-Sun** **galatamuseodelmare.it**

Intrinsic to the revival of Genoa's port area, this museum of the sea is the largest museum of its kind in the Mediterranean region. The complex combines 16th-century and Neo-Classical architecture with a stylish glass, wood and aluminium structure. It is located in the Darsena port area, alongside the Stazione Marittima and the historic Galata shipyards.

The museum illustrates Genoa's longstanding relationship with the sea, from the Middle Ages to the present. Four floors of exhibition space narrate the story of sailing and navigation through exhibits, permanent collections and interactive experiences.

The highlight is a beautifully restored 16th-century Genoese galley, which is lit up at night and visible across the whole bay. Along with a fine display of maps and sailing instruments, the museum houses an original 17th-century launching berth and a reconstructed 17th-century pirate ship, which visitors can board.

A tour of Nazario Sauro, moored in the dock in front of the Galata, is a must to learn about the fascinating world of submarines. Fully interactive, the museum enables visitors to experience life at sea.

← Globe at the innovative maritime museum, Galata Museo del Mare

Frescoes and paintings ↑ adorning the walls at Villa del Principe

14

Villa del Principe

B3 **Piazza del Principe 4** **Principe** **10am-6pm daily** **Public holidays** **doriapamphilj.it**

Constructed for Andrea Doria when he was at the height of his political power, this palazzo was conceived as a truly magnificent, princely residence, a demonstration of the admiral's power. It is still owned by the Doria Pamphilj Trust.

The building was constructed around 1529 and incorporated several existing buildings. When Charles V arrived as a guest in 1533, the decoration was largely complete. The principal artist was Perin del Vaga (c. 1501–47), a pupil of Raphael summoned to Genoa by Andrea Doria.

A marble entrance by Silvio Cosini gives way to an atrium, decorated with frescoes by Perin del Vaga, showing *Stories of the kings of Rome and Military Triumphs*.

On the upper floor, between the public rooms, the Loggia degli Eroi has a stuccoed ceiling by del Vaga and Luzio Romano. Along the internal wall, frescoes by del Vaga depict 12 ancestors of the Doria family. Following lengthy restoration work in the loggia, the splendour of the frescoes' original colours has been greatly revived. The Salone dei Giganti has a ceiling fresco by del Vaga showing *Giants struck by Jove*. Fine tapestries depicting the *Battle of Lepanto*, in the galleria, were made in Brussels in 1591 to a design by Luca Cambiaso.

Around the palazzo, from the water's edge to Monte Granarolo to the rear, there was an enchanting garden, much altered in the 19th and 20th centuries to make way for a section of railway line and several road junctions. Damage during World War II did not help, but there is now a project to return the garden to its 16th-century appearance. The garden's two main landmarks are the Fontana del Tritone by Montorsoli and the Fontana di Nettuno by Taddeo Carlone – both made in the 16th century. The nearby Stazione Marittima, a 1930s departure point for transatlantic liners, was created out of the Dorias' private quay. It is the main hub for ferries, with frequent connections to Cagliari in Sardinia and Palermo in Sicily.

ANDREA DORIA

A member of one of the most powerful families in Genoa, Andrea Doria (1466-1560) was an important figure of Genoese Renaissance history. He made a successful career through warfare: initially serving the pope, then the king of France and, finally, emperor Charles V. A soldier and admiral of huge talent, he was one of the few to defeat feared pirates operating in the Mediterranean. He gained the deep respect of the Genoese, who declared him lord of the city in 1528. From this position of power, he established an aristocratic constitution that lasted until 1798. In his life, Doria single-handedly changed Genoa's history by allying with Spain, bringing the city huge wealth. He spent many years in Villa del Principe, which was built with the help of some of the era's greatest artists.

A SHORT WALK

AROUND VIA GARIBALDI

Distance 1 km (0.5 miles) **Time** 10 minutes
Nearest metro Darsena

When Via Garibaldi was laid out in the mid-16th century, it was the first of the "new streets", and was known as La Strada Nuova. The mansions lining the street are wonderfully preserved, with lavish interiors, and often contain exceptional decoration or art collections – the fruits of shrewd collecting. Among the palazzi open to the public are Palazzo Doria-Tursi, Palazzo Bianco and Palazzo Rosso, which collectively comprise the Musei di Strada Nuova, the city's largest art gallery. Not far away is the first cathedral of Genoa, and the church of San Siro. Enjoy a leisurely stroll, making the most of the fully pedestrianized street.

The church of **San Siro** (p84) *was rebuilt in the late 16th century after a fire. It now features marble inlay and frescoes.*

Palazzo Rosso (p80) *has a gallery with treasures such as portraits by Van Dyck and Genoese works from the 16th to the 18th centuries.*

VIA SAN SIRO

VIA CAIROLI

START

PIAZZA MERIDIANA

VIA DELLA MADDALENA

Did You Know?

The French writer Madame de Staël was so in awe of Via Garibaldi that she dubbed it the "street of kings".

Palazzo Bianco (p82) *houses a gallery with 13th- to 18th-century European paintings, including a large number of Genoese, Spanish, French and Flemish works.*

← Strolling past a picturesque sidewalk café on Via Garibaldi

The 16th-century **Palazzo Doria-Tursi** *(p83) is three times the length of the other mansions in Via Garibaldi. It features a lovely courtyard and an arcaded loggia.*

0 metres   50   N
0 yards   50   ↑

Palazzo del Podestà
was begun in 1563. The façade is a delightful example of Genoese Mannerism.

Via Garibaldi, *with its monumental façades, transports visitors back to the heyday of the Genoese aristocracy.*

Villa del Principe *(p88) has a Baroque façade dating from 1563–67.*

Palazzo Carrega Cataldi *is home to the Chamber of Commerce.*

VIA GARIBALDI

PIAZZA FONTANE MAROSE

FINISH

PIAZZA D. FERRO

Must Sees

BEYOND THE CENTRE

Genoa sprawls westwards and eastwards from the city centre, running up to the old city walls. These walls, built in the 17th century, circle the regional capital some distance from the Centro Storico and feature magnificent fortresses still in a perfect state of preservation. Since the creation of Greater Genoa in the 1920s, when 19 additional municipalities were annexed to the city, the area beyond the centre has become remarkably varied: the residential district of Albaro to the east is full of elegant villas, while Boccadasse is a quiet fishing village, and Nervi is a famous resort with beautiful Art Nouveau buildings.

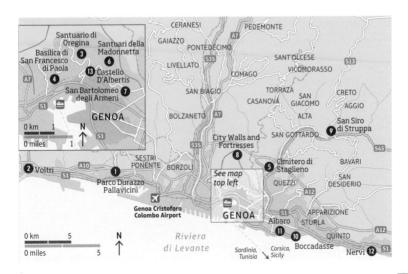

↑ The Temple of Diana and a Chinese pagoda, sitting on the park's biggest lake

1 PARCO DURAZZO PALLAVICINI

Via Pallavicini 13, Pegli ⏰**Botanical Gardens: 9:30am–7pm Tue–Fri, 10am–7pm Sat & Sun (Oct & Mar: to 6pm); guided tours: hours vary, check website** 🌐**villadurazzopallavicini.it**

The beautiful landscaped gardens of the Villa Durazzo Pallavicini, spreading over 11 ha (27 acres) in the town of Pegli, are among the finest in Italy. Today, more than 100 varieties of rare species, including tropical carnivorous plants, are grown here.

Michele Canzio, set designer at Genoa's Teatro Carlo Felice (*p66*), was responsible for transforming the gardens of the Villa Durazzo Pallavicini. Between 1837 and 1846, he created a splendid English-style garden, following the romantic fashion of the time. He was commissioned by Marchese Ignazio Alessandro Pallavicini, who inherited the villa from his aunt Clelia Pallavicini Durazzo. She was passionate about plants and had begun a botanic garden here in the late 18th century.

Canzio designed the park as a stage for a historical fairy tale, whose story unwinds en route through the grounds. The narrative consists of a prologue, made up of the Gothic Avenue and the Classic Avenue, and three acts, which tie together the park's sights and end at the Temple of Flora.

Did You Know?

The park has the largest collection of camellia flowers in Italy.

Mausoleum of the Captain

This 14th-century castle was conceived as the house of a lord of the time.

↑ Parco Durazzo Pallavicini and its many architectural marvels

WHAT ELSE TO SEE IN PEGLI

A popular retreat for the Genoese, Pegli was a holiday destination for aristocrats from the end of the 19th century. Two villas hint at its former elegance. Villa Durazzo Pallavicini is the home of the archaeology museum, Museo Civico di Archeologia Ligure *(www.museidigenova. it)*. Villa Centurione Doria houses the Museo Civico Navale *(www. museonavale.it)*, which traces Genoa's rich seafaring history.

Cappelletta della Madonna

The Triumphal Arch features reliefs and statues by Giovanni Battista Cevasco.

The Chinese Pagoda's roof has little bells and sculpted dragons.

Coffee house

Swiss chalet

The Temple of Diana is an Ionic-style temple dedicated to the Graeco-Roman goddess of hunting. A statue of Diana by Giovanni Battista Cevasco is beneath the dome, surrounded by four tritons.

The Temple of Flora, dedicated to the Roman goddess of flowers, is an impressive octagonal building surrounded by box hedges.

EXPERIENCE MORE

②

Voltri

FS Genoa-Savona line 🚌

One of the most important towns in Greater Genoa, Voltri is more or less a continuation of the periphery of the city. Villa Brignole-Sale, originally built in the 17th century and also known as the Villa della Duchessa di Galliera, is a highlight of this town. In 1870, the palace became the home of Maria Brignole-Sale, Duchess of Galliera. Her most striking

---

💬 INSIDER TIP
Walk the Tracks

The 16-km (10-mile) coastal path from Voltri to Varazze is a scenic paved route that traces an old railway line. If you don't feel like walking back, you can hop on a train for the return journey.

---

contribution was the creation of an English-style garden, complete with pine trees, holm oaks and a deer park.

The park extends for more than 32 ha (80 acres) and is scattered with romantic follies and farmhouses. The villa is not open to the public, but the vast grounds, known as the **Parco Storico Villa Duchessa di Galliera,** are open and are worth exploring. Within the villa's grounds, you can take a guided tour of the vast agricultural estates upon which some of the region's finest wines were once grown. At the end of the tour, wine tastings are offered, including samples of the Bordeaux "Mouton Cadet" and the Chateau Haut Monteils. Other themed walks and talks are offered in the summer season. Tickets and times are available through the park's website.

On the left of the villa stands the grand Sanctuary of Nostra Signora delle Grazie. The Duchess of Galliera had

it restored in opulent Gothic style. She was buried here in 1888.

Parco Storico Villa Duchessa di Galliera
🚲 🏠 Voltri ⏰ 8am-7:30pm daily 🌐 villaduchessa digalliera.it

---

③

Santuario di Oregina

🏠 Salita Oregina 44 ☎ 010 212024 🚌 39, 40 ⏰ 8am-noon & 4-7pm daily 🚫 Sun & Aug pm

Overlooking the city and the sea, this sanctuary stands at the top of a flight of steps in a scenic setting. Its history is linked with the worship of the Madonna di Loreto.

A group of monks chose this area as a place of hermitage in 1634. The monks immediately built a simple chapel here, but this was taken over by the Franciscan Friars Minor the following year.

> **The Basilica di San Francesco di Paola is at one end of the Circonvallazione a Monte, the panoramic road that snakes across the slopes just above the city.**

The sanctuary as it appears today was built in 1650–55, with further modifications being made in 1707, including the addition of a dome and changes to the façade.
The upper part of the façade has pilasters, Corinthian columns, a large window and a curvilinear pediment with stuccoes, following the dictates of Ligurian Baroque churches in hilly areas.

Inside the sanctuary, the painting *St Joseph with Baby Jesus*, by Andrea Carlone, is a highlight. There are also mementoes of the Risorgimento era, including the funerary monument of Alessandro de Stefanis. Born in Savona in 1826, de Stefanis fought against Piedmontese troops following Napoleon's decision to give Genoa to the King of Piedmont (*p47*). He died in Genoa in 1849 and is now revered as a local hero. The church is also famous for its nativity scene (*presepe*), which dates back to the 1700s.

4

Basilica di San Francesco di Paola

🏛 Salita San Francesco di Paola 44 📞 010 261 228 🚌 32, 35 🕙 Apr–Sep: 7:30am–noon & 3:30–7pm daily; Oct–Mar: 7:30am–noon & 3:30–6pm daily

This sanctuary is at one end of the Circonvallazione a Monte, the panoramic road that snakes across the slopes just above the city. From the church courtyard, built on a rocky outcrop that dominates the district of Fassolo, visitors can enjoy a marvellous view of Genoa's Porto Antico, which can be reached via a brick-paved road lined with the Stations of the Cross. The basilica played an important role in the 17th century, when its patrons included powerful families such as the Doria, the Balbi and the Spinola. Also known as the Sanctuary of Sailors, the church has numerous mariners' ex votos. In the third chapel on the right is a *Nativity* by Luca Cambiaso, while the chapel at the end of the left aisle has a *Washing of the Feet* signed by Orazio De Ferrari. Anton Maria Maragliano, one of the most active sculptors in Liguria in the 17th century, designed the statue of the Virgin Mary in the apse.

EAT

Priano
This family-run bakery and pastry shop is best known for its focaccia.

🏛 Via Carlo Camozzini 76 R 🌐 priano.info

€ € €

Ostaia da U Santu
A laid-back osteria serving home-cooked fare including *cappon magro*, a lavish seafood and vegetable salad.

🏛 Via Al Santuario delle Grazie 33 🌐 ostaiadausantu.it

€ € €

Trattoria Lemerle
Enjoy seasonal plates celebrating local vegetables and fresh seafood.

🏛 Via Carlo Camozzini 142 🌐 ostaiadausantu.it

€ € €

← The Villa Duchessa di Galliera in Voltri seen from the vast grounds

Walking though the lower portico at Cimitero di Staglieno, and *(inset)* tombstones in the upper portico

⑤
Cimitero di Staglieno

🏠 Piazzale Resasco 1 🚌 12, 14, 34, 48 🕐 7:30am-5pm daily (25 Dec & Easter: to 1pm) 🚫 1 & 6 Jan, Easter Mon, 24 Jun, 15 Aug, 26 Dec 🌐 comunegenova.it

This vast and extraordinary Neo-Classical cemetery on the bank of the River Bisagno, northeast of the city centre, was designed by Carlo Barabino, who died before the grand project was carried out (1844–51). The cemetery fills an area of 160 ha (395 acres), hence the shuttle bus which ferries people around.

In a dominant position at the heart of the cemetery stands the Cappella dei Suffragi, adorned with statues by Cevasco, sculptor of the statues in the Parco Durazzo Pallavicini (p94). Other notable works include the colossal 19th-century marble statue of *Faith* by Santo Varni, and, probably the best-known monument at Staglieno, the tomb of Giuseppe Mazzini, the great philosopher of the Risorgimento. Also buried here, in the Protestant section, is Constance Mary Lloyd, wife of Oscar Wilde.

⑥
Santuario della Madonnetta

🏠 Salita della Madonnetta 5 📞 010 272 5308 🚋 Zecca-Righi funicular 🚌 39 🕐 4-6pm Mon-Fri, 10am-noon Sat, Sun & hols

Lying at the end of a *creuza*, one of Liguria's distinctive steep narrow streets, paved with brick, this sanctuary is one of the highlights along the Circonvallazione a Monte.

The complex Baroque building was erected in 1696 for the Augustine Order. The delightful area paved with black and white pebbles outside dates from the 18th century. On one side, a niche contains a marble sculpture of a *Pietà* by Domenico Parodi.

The interior is also charming, with a light-filled central chamber in the form of an irregular octagon, linked to the presbytery by two side staircases. Another ramp leads beneath the presbytery down to the "*scurolo*", an underground chamber on whose altar stands a revered 17th-century statue of the *Madonnetta*, from which the sanctuary takes its name – it is the work of Giovanni Romano. In the chapel alongside is a wooden *Pietà*, by Anton Maria Maragliano.

The sanctuary's crypt houses some of Genoa's best-loved nativity scenes *(presepi)*, of particular interest because of their faithful reproduction of parts of the old city centre.

In the sacristy, visitors can see an interesting rendition of the 15th-century *Annunciation*, attributed to Ludovico Brea (p168), a celebrated native of Nice who was active in Ligurian artitsic circles from around 1475 to 1520.

❼

San Bartolomeo degli Armeni

🏛 Piazza San Bartolomeo degli Armeni 2 ☎ 010 839 2496 🚌 36 & 49 ⏰ Mass: 5:30pm Mon–Sun (also 11am Sun)

This church was founded in 1308 by Basilian monks (followers of St Basil), and then passed to the Barnabites, who rebuilt it in 1775 and are the current occupants. The church is almost completely enclosed by a 19th-century building, but still has its bell tower, dating from 1300.

San Bartolomeo owes its fame to the fact that it is home to the relic of Santo Volto (Holy Face), a piece of linen with an image of the face of Jesus Christ. People also call it "Santo Sudario", or "Mandillo" (handkerchief in the local dialect). This relic was given to Leonardo Montaldo, doge of Genoa, in 1362 by the Byzantine emperor Giovanni V Paleologo, in return for military assistance. The doge, in turn, gave the relic to the Basilian monks.

The Santo Volto itself is set against a background of gold and silver filigree (a masterpiece of Byzantine goldsmithery), with ten embossed tiles describing the origins of the portrait and later episodes in its history. The most valuable work of art is the triptych on the high altar, *Madonna and Saints*, by Turino Vanni.

---

❽ Ⓜ

City Walls and Fortresses

🏛 Parco Urbano della Mura 🚆 Genova-Casella line 🚌 40 🚠 Zecca-Righi 🌐 ferroviagenovacasella.it

Genoa's defensive walls have been rebuilt or moved several times over the centuries. Traces remain of the 1155 and 1536 walls, but the impressive 13-km (8-mile) triangle of walls that still encloses the city dates from the 1600s. These fortifications, which became known as La Nuova Mura ("the New Wall"), were designed in part by Bartolomeo Bianco, and became one of the city's outstanding features.

The best way to explore the old walls is to drive along the scenic Strada delle Mura, which begins at Piazza Manin, north of the Centro Storico, and follows the line of what remains of the 17th-century walls. Piazza Manin itself is home to the fanciful Castello Mackenzie (1893–1905), the work of Gino Coppedè, which embraces medieval, Renaissance and even Art Nouveau influences.

Travelling along the line of the walls in an anti-clockwise direction, you reach Forte Castellaccio, rebuilt in the 16th century by Andrea Doria, and again altered in the 1830s. Within its ring of bastions is the Torre della Specola, where condemned men were once hanged.

Forte Sperone juts out on the top of Monte Peralto, at the apex of the triangle. Originally 16th-century, the massive citadel seen today was built in 1826–7 by the House of Savoy.

THE CASELLA TRAIN

The Genoa-Casella line is one of the few narrow-gauge railway tracks remaining in Italy. It takes 55 minutes to make the 24-km (15-mile) journey from Piazza Manin past the city walls into the Apennine hinterland. The route passes forests and reaches its highest point at Crocetta, the ancient border of the Genoese Republic.

Inland from Forte Sperone, off the line of the city walls, lies Forte Puin (accessible by train from the Genoa–Casella line), completed in 1828. Its square tower is one of the key landmarks in the Parco Urbano delle Mura. Polygonal Forte Diamante, the furthest inland of the forts, is in a high and delightful position. Dating from 1758, it has survived almost intact.

Forte Tenaglia, which dominates the Valle del Polcevera, was first recorded in the 16th century. The building's horn-shaped structure, acquired in the 19th century, was badly damaged in World War II.

↑ Vines growing on the 16th-century Forte Sperone, part of the city walls

❾ San Siro di Struppa

📍 Via di Creto 64 📞 010 809 000 🚌 12, 14 🕘 9am–7pm daily

This abbey church sits in an isolated position among pretty gardens and rows of vines in the district of Struppa, the most north easterly part of Genoa. Mentioned in 13th-century documents, it was built around 1000 and named after the bishop of Genoa, San Siro, who was born here in the 4th century. From the late 16th century onwards, the church was tampered with periodically, by the end of which its early Romanesque appearance had greatly suffered. Separate projects to restore the building have restored San Siro to its original form, including the restoration of the decorative masonry in grey sandstone and the pavement of black and white pebbles outside the church.

The façade, pierced by a rose window, is divided by pilasters into three sections that correspond to the three interior aisles. Above is a bell tower, with three-mullioned windows at the top.

Inside the abbey, traces of the original fresco decoration are still visible, and the columns in the nave feature interesting capitals. On the wall in the right-hand aisle is a gilded wooden statue of San Siro, dating from 1640 and much restored.

The splendid *Polyptych of San Siro* (depicting the saint enthroned, eight scenes from his life and the Virgin and Child) dates from 1516. It is possibly the work of Pier Francesco Sacchi and hangs in the left-hand aisle.

> **Inside San Siro di Struppa, traces of the fresco decoration are still visible, and the columns in the nave feature interesting capitals.**

❿ Boccadasse

🚌

At the start of the Riviera di Levante, but still within Greater Genoa, Boccadasse is a fishing village which has managed to retain its picturesque charm. The houses (their façades painted in lively colours), are tightly packed around the small harbour. This is one of the most popular destinations for the Genoese, who come here for day trips, especially at weekends.

⓫ Albaro

🚌

Albaro was one of the towns annexed to the city in 1926. It marks the start of the eastern, Levante zone of Greater Genoa, an almost unbroken succession of settlements, rich in both artistic and historical interest, extending as far as Nervi. The scenic Corso d'Italia road hugs the coast along the way.

Since the Middle Ages, Albaro has been a popular spot for Genoa's high nobility to build their country houses. It remains the city's residential district par excellence. Though now rather over-developed, it has a series of beautiful suburban villas. One of these is the 16th-century Villa Saluzzo Bombrini, also known as "il Paradiso". Its charming Renaissance garden features in *Trattenimento in un Giardino di Albaro*, the famous painting by Alessandro Magnasco, now in Palazzo Bianco (*p82*).

Villa Saluzzo Mongiardino, dating from the early 18th century, played host to the English poet Lord Byron in 1823. Villa Giustinani Cambiaso is the work of the great Renaissance architect Galeazzo Alessi, and was highly influential at the time. Set in an elevated position, surrounded by extensive grounds, it now houses the university's faculty of engineering. Inside are decorative reliefs that are reminiscent of Classicism and Roman Mannerism. Two frescoes by the Bergamo artist Gian Battista Castello and Luca Cambiaso embellish the upstairs loggia.

⓬ Nervi

FS 🚌 W nervi.ge.it

Nervi was, from the second half of the 19th century, a major holiday destination

↑ Lights illuminating the fishing village of Boccadasse at dawn

⚲ GREAT VIEW
Passeggiata Anita Garibaldi

With views along Nervi's rocky shore and across the entire Riviera di Levante as far as Monte di Portofino, Passeggiata Anita Garibaldi offers one of the most beautiful panoramas in Italy.

for the European aristocracy, especially the English. These days it is better known for its international dance festival, held in the summer.

The town's seaside location, gardens and art are the main attractions. The 2-km (1-mile) Passeggiata Anita Garibaldi, the path created for the mayor Marchese Gaetano Gropallo, passes the 16th-century Torre Gropallo, which was later modified by the Marchese in Neo-Medieval style.

Villa Gropallo houses the town library, while Villa Serra has the **Galleria d'Arte Moderna**, a gallery with a fine gathering of Ligurian paintings from the last two centuries.

The **Wolfsonian Museum** was donated to the city by American philanthropist Mitchell "Micky" Wolfson, Jr. Exhibits focus mainly on decorative arts from the first half of the 20th century.

Galleria d'Arte Moderna

⌂ Villa Serra, Via Capolungo 3 ☎ 010 557 6976 ⌚ 11am-6pm Tue-Fri, noon-7pm Sat & Sun

Wolfsonian Museum

⌂ Via Serra Gropallo 4 ☎ 010 557 5595 ⌚ 11am-6pm Tue-Fri, noon-7pm Sat & Sun
🌐 museidigenova.it

13 🖊️

Castello D'Albertis

⌂ Corso Dogali 18 🚌 39, 40 ⌚ Apr-Sep: 10am-6pm Tue-Sun (Sat & Sun: to 7pm); Oct-Mar: 10am-5pm Tue-Sun (Sat & Sun: to 6pm)
🌐 museidigenova.it

This fortress, built in just six years from 1886 to 1892, occupies a striking position on the bastion of Montegalletto, not far from the city centre. The man behind the building was captain Enrico Alberto D'Albertis, a curious figure who was a courageous explorer and navigator. He was passionate about the project and employed a group of four architects, under the leadership of Alfredo D'Andrade, the great exponent of the Neo-Gothic revival of that time.

One of the most emblematic symbols of revivalism in Genoa, Castello D'Albertis stands out for the beauty of its Neo-Gothic complex – from its mighty 16th-century base to its battlemented towers. The terracotta cladding echoes a style used in similar Genoese Romanesque monuments.

The captain bequeathed the building to the town council in 1932, together with the ethnographic collections that are on display in the Museo Etnografico that now occupies the castle. Among items left by the captain are several sundials (made by D'Albertis himself), nautical instruments and geographical publications, as well as arms from that era. The museum also received a donation of finds from the American Committee of Catholic Missions in 1892. This donation included clothing of Indigenous peoples, crafts and jewellery and terracotta pieces, masks, stone sculptures and vases dating from the Mayan and Aztec civilizations. Other acquisitions include objects from South-east Asia, Oceania and New Guinea.

→ The fine exterior of the Neo-Gothic Castello D'Albertis

EXPERIENCE THE ITALIAN RIVIERA

The tiny port of Riomaggiore

THE RIVIERA DI LEVANTE

The Riviera di Levante occupies the wild coastal stretch between the capital of Genoa to the west and the border with Tuscany to the south. The region has been inhabited since prehistoric times, though the Levante's undulating landscapes have long made it difficult terrain for human habitation.

The Roman colony of Portus Lunae was founded in 177 BCE, and the Levante became a major port for the shipping of marble. As Genoa rose inexorably as a maritime power from the beginning of the 12th century, the towns along the coast revolted against incorporation into the unofficial Genoese republic. The struggle was ultimately in vain, however, and by 1232 the entire Riviera di Levante was under Genoese control.

In the following centuries, agriculture and wine-making became key to the Levante's fortunes, and the area's dry white wines had built a considerable reputation by the 16th century. To maintain the vines and fruit trees meant continuously terracing the rolling hills using dry stone walls, a feat of engineering still used today.

Tourism has thrived in the area since the 1800s, with new railway links making the Levante's remote villages accessible to larger crowds. While this drives the local economy, centuries of formidable visitor numbers have resulted in severe overtourism in some areas, particularly around the popular Cinque Terre.

LOMBARDY

Vignole
Borbera

Rocchetta
Ligure

Casale Staffora

Gavi

PIEDMONT

Isola del
Cantone

S145

Mongiardino
Ligure

S147

S18

Carrosio

Cabella
Ligure

S45

Voltaggio

Crocefieschi

A7

Monte Antola
1,597 m (5,239 ft)

Ottone

RIVIERA DI
PONENTE
p134

Chiesa
Giovi

San Bartolomeo

Parco Regionale del Monte Antola

Pentema

Lago del
Brugneto

Montebruno

San Quirico

GENOA
p50

S35

S226

Montoggio

8 TORRIGLIA

LIGURIA

Diamante

Struppa

S45

Appennino

Parazzuolo

D586

A10

A7

Pegli

Genova
(Genoa)

A12

S225

Cicagna

Borzonasca

Genoa Cristoforo
Colombo Airport

S1

Nervi

Uscio

Lavagna

5 BOGLIASCO

S1

Recco

A12

Carasco

S225

Ligurian
Sea

6 CAMOGLI

Golfo di
Paradiso

9 RAPALLO

Zoagli

San Fruttuoso

7

SANTA MARGHERITA
LIGURE

Chiavari **11** CHIAVARI

1

Portofino

14

PORTOFINO
PENINSULA

Golfo di
Tigullio

LAVAGNA

S1

SESTRI
LEVANTE **15**

Punta
Manara

↓ Porto Torres,
Tunisia

RIVIERA DI
LEVANTE

↘ Palermo

THE RIVIERA DI LEVANTE

Must Sees
1. Portofino Peninsula
2. The Cinque Terre
3. La Spezia
4. Sarzana

Experience More
5. Bogliasco
6. Camogli
7. Santa Margharita Ligure
8. Torriglia
9. Rapallo
10. Santa Stefano d'Aveto
11. Chiavari
12. Abbazia di Sant'Andrea di Borzone
13. Bonassola
14. Lavagna
15. Sestri Lavante
16. Varese Ligure
17. Palmaria, Tino and Tinetto
18. Portovenere
19. Levanto
20. Campiglia
21. Luni
22. Ameglia
23. Bocca di Magra
24. Castelnuovo Magra
25. San Terenzo
26. Lerici
27. Montemarcello
28. Fiascherino and Tellaro

❶

PORTOFINO PENINSULA

🅰 E4 🅰 Genoa 🚉🚌 Santa Margherita Ligure ⛴ Boats around the Golfo del Tigullio and to Cinque Terre (Apr–Sep); www.navigazione golfodeipoeti.net 🎫 Via Roma 35; www.portofinotourism.com

This stunning headland to the east of Genoa, with its high cliffs, Mediterranean maquis and woods of chestnut trees, is dotted with picturesque hamlets with luxury hotels and countless scenic hiking trails. The large dolphin population is one of the main attractions here, as are the many maritime sports available, which include some of Liguria's very best diving.

① Portofino

🚌🚏 🎫 Portofino: Piazza Martiri dell'Olivetta; Parco Naturale Regionale di Portofino: Viale Rainusso 1, www.parcoportofino.it

Until the start of the 20th century, Portofino was a quiet fishing village. This changed as tourism boomed in the 1950s, when the village became popular for its calm waters and scenic harbour. Still busy with global tourists, older buildings have now been transformed into fashionable boutique hotels and chic restaurants.

The cove around Portofino is sheltered by its secure coastal position and by a 600-m (1,970-ft) mountain range that forms a 3-km (2-mile) long cliff behind the town. The resort is surrounded by the Parco Naturale Regionale di Portofino, founded in 1935, with the striking castle, Castello Brown, looming over the harbour. The protected parkland encompasses an array of landscapes with nine mountains within its borders, the highest being Monte di Portofino at 616 m (2,021 ft).

TOURIST FINES

Portofino introduced no-waiting zones in 2023 to combat the town's increasing tourist congestion. Though the town has only 400 residents, it is thronged with tourists in the high season, causing overcrowded streets and long traffic jams. Visitors caught taking photographs on the busy quay between 10:30am and 6pm risk a fine of €270.

Fortezza di San Giorgio, known as "Castello Brown", is a 16th-century fortress.

← The rocky Portofino Peninsula

Punta di Portofino features a lighthouse and the Madonnina del Capo statue.

TOP 4 WALKS NEAR PORTOFINO

Camogli to San Rocco
Take the 4-km (2.5-mile) hike from Camogli *(p122)* along the ocean-hugging Via San Rocco.

Camogli to San Fruttuoso
This 6-km (3.5-mile) route to San Fruttuoso *(p111)* passes through verdant olive groves.

Santa Margherita to Paraggi
A 1.5-km (0.8-mile) track leads from the valley of Paraggi *(p110)* to Santa Margherita.

Passeggiata dei Baci
The "Walk of Kisses" is a popular, easy 8.5-km (5-mile) trail around the beautiful inlets of Portofino harbour.

← Portofino harbour, and *(inset)* the Passeggiata dei Baci, which links Paraggi and Portofino

SHOP

Ferragamo
Shop luxury Italian footwear, designer handbags and stylish accessories at this high-end retailer.

🏠 Piazza Martiri dell'Olivetta 13
📞 0185 267 057

Loro Piana
This charming boutique of the Italian brand Loro Piana offers high-quality clothes, including personalized fits. An excellent tailoring service is also available.

🏠 Piazza Martiri dell'Olivetta 9
🌐 loropiana.com

Spinnaker Boutique
Chic clothes and fashion items, including accessories and bags, are sold in a lavishly decorated and welcoming environment at this store.

🏠 Calata Marconi 29
🌐 spinnakerboutique.it

DIOR Paraggi
The crowning jewel of Portofino Peninsula's high-end retailers, DIOR Paraggi's luxurious clothes, bags and shoes are matched by the store's equally sumptuous interior.

🏠 Lungomare Paraggi, Via Paraggi
📞 0185 215 379

↑ The Bay of Paraggi, with its crystal-clear blue waters

②
Paraggi

🍽

In Paraggi, a short distance from Portofino, bright, multi-coloured houses are gathered around a small sandy cove, with terraces rising up the mountain behind. Nowadays, the once-flourishing trades of fishing and olive pressing have given way to tourism. The views from here are beautiful.

The beach at Baia di Paraggi is the only sandy beach on the otherwise rocky Portofino peninsula, with strikingly clear blue waters. It is a deservedly popular place to relax, but local companies charge very large sums to rent chairs and umbrellas, and parking near the beaches can be extortionate. It is suggested that visitors travel on foot from Portofino, following the short 2-km (1-mile) trail that hugs the headland.

→ The beach of San Fruttuoso, beneath its imposing abbey

> Every year, on the last Sunday in July, garlands of flowers are given to the Cristo degli Abissi statue in memory of those who have lost their lives at sea.

③

San Fruttuoso

🚲 🚹 **Abbey of San Fruttuoso: Via S Fruttuoso 13; 0185 772 703; hours vary, call ahead**

A symbol of the Italian heritage and conservation organization FAI, to which it has belonged since 1983, San Fruttuoso is a delightful village with houses grouped around a Benedictine abbey, built by the Doria family in the 1200s. For centuries, sailors would anchor their boats beneath the abbey and unload their wares directly into its cellars. The abbey has a striking octagonal bell tower. Alongside is the cloister and mausoleum of the Doria family. San Fruttuoso is accessible only by boat or on foot: it is 30 minutes by boat from Camogli, for example,

or 75 minutes' walk from Portofino. The nearest parking to San Fruttuoso is around Camogli *(p122)*, where numerous waymarked trails lead through the Parco Naturale Regionale di Portofino towards the village.

④

Cristo degli Abissi (Christ of the Abyss)

🅿 **Portofino** 🚲

This bronze statue was created by Italian sculptor Guido Galletti. The statue was lowered into the sea at San Fruttuoso in 1954, designed as a symbol of the attachment of the Ligurian people to the sea. Every year, on the last Sunday in July, garlands of flowers are given to the statue in memory of those who have

🔺 GREAT VIEW
Gaze Across the Italian Riviera

Catch a ferry to San Fruttuoso from Portofino for stunning views of the coast. Golfo Paradiso *(www.golfo paradiso.it/tourist-lines)* offers regular ferries around the Peninsula.

lost their lives at sea. Divers pay homage to the statue at all times of the year. The statue undergoes regular underwater cleaning to prevent erosion, and is sporadically hauled out of the sea for more thorough renovations.

② 🎨

THE CINQUE TERRE

🅰 F5 🚉 ℹ La Spezia station; 0187 185 7573

Located along the rocky coastline of the Riviera di Levante, the Cinque Terre comprises five villages: Monterosso al Mare, Vernazza, Corniglia, Manarola and Riomaggiore. Clinging dramatically to the steep cliffs, these villages are linked by an ancient footpath known as the Sentiero Azzurro (Blue Path), which offers spectacular views of the rocky coastline and terraced vineyards that produce the local dry white wines. The footpath also provides access to secluded beaches. The best way to tour the villages is by boat or by train.

①

Monterosso al Mare

🚉 Monterosso al Mare station; 0187 185 7573

Monterosso, the westernmost village of the Cinque Terre, is the largest and most resort-like of the five villages. It is also the most accessible (being slightly less vertical and having fewer steps than the other villages), so is the best choice for visitors with limited mobility or small children. The village is made up of two distinct parts: the "new town" of Fegina and the "old town" of Monterosso Vecchio. While the beach, train station and much of the tourist accommodation is located in Fegina, hotels, restaurants and shops, as well as the village's nightlife scene, are found nearby in Monterosso Vecchio.

Visitors are largely drawn to Monterosso Vecchio's ancient medieval centre and to the long stretch of sandy beach (the only extensive beach in the Cinque Terre). The beach (which is free) fills up especially fast. There are other private beaches in the vicinity, entry to some of which must be booked in advance (these private beaches close at 5pm).

The historical centre of Monterosso is crammed with picture-perfect houses, artisan shops and tiny winding passageways. Soak up the

> 💬 INSIDER TIP
> **Best Time to Visit the Villages**
>
> The best time to visit the beautiful Cinque Terre for hiking and swimming is from mid-April to mid-October, but avoid August, when hotel prices skyrocket and the hiking trails and beaches become very crowded.

Pastel-coloured houses perched on the cliffside at Manarola

atmosphere while exploring the village's network of cobbled streets, stopping at one of the local wine cellars for a glass of delicious Sciacchetrà (a sweet wine produced in the fertile hills of the Cinque Terre). When you've finished exploring the streets, head to Torre Aurora on the waterfront, a 13th-century tower that was formerly part of the village's wider fortifications (the other towers have been demolished over the past two centuries). Not far from Torre Aurora, you'll find a small monastery. It offers views over the town and across the wider Cinque Terre.

Monterosso al Mare's main square, Piazza Garibaldi – home of busy cafés, the town hall and a statue of Garibaldi – is a wonderful spot for people-watching. Also of note is the beautiful Church of San Francesco near the square, with its impressive collection of artistic treasures, which include a crucifixion attributed to Van Dyck. Another site of interest, a short walk from Piazza Garibaldi, is the holiday home of Eugenio Montale (Nobel-prize winning Italian poet), who used the Cinque Terre as inspiration for many of his works.

②
Manarola

🚉 **Manarola station; 0187 760 515**

Clinging to a cliff overlooking the sea, the village of Manarola is a strikingly beautiful sight with its compact, colourful houses rising up from the sea. It marks the beginning of the famous Via dell'Amore ("The Way of Love") footpath, an easy-to-walk, 2-km (1.2-mile) paved path connecting Manarola to Riomaggiore. The path is called the "Way of Love" because it provided easy passage for young lovers who lived in the two towns.

Other Manarola attractions include the Church of San Lorenzo, located in the upper part of the village. A richly decorated Gothic edifice, it features a rose window dating back to the 14th century. A 14th-century oratory and a 13th century bell tower can be found nearby. The Punta Bonfiglio viewpoint, a 10-minute walk away, offers views along the whole coastline.

Manarola's marina doubles as a sunbathing and swimming spot from morning until dusk. The marina's stone jetties are the perfect place from which to dive into the calm waters.

TOP 3 BEACHES NEAR MONTEROSSO

Monterosso Beach, Old Town
Situated close to the station in Monterosso's Old Town, this scenic beach offers tranquil sea views.

Monterosso Beach, Fegina
This beautiful sandy beach has plenty of free areas for towels if you don't want to rent a bed.

Vernazza Beach
The waters here remain calm, making this the perfect place for a leisurely swim.

③

Vernazza

🏠 ℹ Vernazza station;
0187 028 316

Vernazza is often regarded as the most beautiful of the five towns and it's not hard to see why. A small harbour nestles under the shadow of the 11th-century Doria castle and a dramatic seaside church, the Santa Margherita di Antiochia. Its charming piazza is framed by tall, pastel-hued buildings and, beyond the town, steeply terraced olive groves crowd the hillsides.

Due to its size and popularity, Vernazza can get extremely crowded during the tourist season (May–September). During this time, it is best to visit

---

🔺 GREAT VIEW
Cinque Terre Panorama

Visit the Belvedere di Santa Maria, a breezy sea-facing terrace with 180-degree views of the Cinque Terre coastline. It's the only place where all five villages can be seen at once.

---

early in the morning or in the evening, when most of the day-trippers have left. The train station is a mere 10-minute walk from the harbour and there are plenty of cafés, shops and places of interest along the route. Get lost in the side streets; take one of the numerous trails that lead away from the village or up to its commanding 16th-century Belforte tower, which offers a fantastic view of the coastline. Hikes to the sanctuaries of San Bernardino and the Madonna della Neveare (trafficked usually only by local farmers) are well worth the effort – visitors will be rewarded with incredible views.

---

④

Corniglia

🏠 ℹ Corniglia station;
0187 185 7573

Corniglia is in the centre of the Cinque Terre, perched on a high promontory and surrounded on three sides by terraced vineyards. It is the smallest village and was the last to succumb to tourism, mainly due to the difficulties visitors encounter

in reaching it. Day-trippers can choose to tackle the 382 steep steps from the waterfront train station or take the shuttle bus that runs from the station. On arrival, visitors will be rewarded with some great places to eat and a number of interesting shops. Wander along the main street and enjoy your focaccia or gelato in the scenic piazzetta.

---

⑤

Riomaggiore

🏠 ℹ Riomaggiore station;
0187 185 7573

Riomaggiore is the nearest village to La Spezia and the unofficial capital of the Cinque Terre. It is divided into two parts by the railway line. The lower part is the fishing village where visitors can watch fishers hauling in the day's catch, or enjoy a delicious seafood feast at one of the restaurants dotted around the small, characteristic port. Surrounded by colourful town houses and with boats lined up along its ramp, it is the Cinque Terre at its best.

Via Colombo, the steep main street, is located in the upper part of the village,

Stores and cafés lining Corniglia's narrow main street, Via Fieschi ↑

→

One of the many scenic paths in Cinque Terre National Park

flanked by terraced vineyards. Here visitors can find a variety of restaurants, bars and souvenir shops, and a piazza in which to take a break from the many steps. Climbing further uphill, visit the Church of San Giovanni Battista and the 13th-century castle, and enjoy wonderful views of the village from both.

⑥ 🏃

Cinque Terre National Park

🌐 www.card.parco nazionale5terre.it

While the Cinque Terre's five villages are undeniably beautiful, the surrounding hills and mountains have their own charm, offering wonders in abundance for hikers. Stretching for 39 sq km (15 sq miles) between Levanto and La Spezia, the Cinque Terre National Park is striking, with terraces supported by dry stone walls weaving around the cliffside. It is the smallest and most densely populated national park in Italy.

The park was established in 1999 in recognition of the area's agricultural,

historical and cultural value. A telling example of the intricate relationship between local communities and their land, this living natural landscape is the result of a deep understanding of the surrounding environment. Here, plots of arable land have been meticulously hand carved into the mountainside, sustaining the community's way of life for over a millennium.

The Cinque Terre National Park is easy to explore, with several trails linking the villages. Due to the high volume of visitors who now walk the park's trails in the summer season, the whole area suffers from severe soil erosion. A dedicated team of grounds-people work tirelessly to ensure the trails are safe and well maintained. The entire park is designated a pedestrian-friendly zone, and, while cars are permitted between the villages, it is highly recommended to arrive at the park by boat or train. From any of the Cinque Terre's villages, waymarked trails point the way into the park, and offer routes for walkers of all abilities.

STAY

Hotel Porto Roca
This charming hotel has an infinity pool, sea views and an excellent on-site restaurant.

🏠 Via Corone 1, Monterosso al Mare 🌐 portoroca.it

€€€

La Malà
A lovely family-run B&B, La Malà offers stunning seaside views.

🏠 Via San Giovanni Battista 29, Vernazza 🌐 lamala.it

€€€

Cinqueterre Residence
One of the more upmarket Cinque Terre hotels, the rooms here come with a hot tub and a free minibar.

🏠 Via de Battè 67, Riomaggiore 🌐 cinque terreresidence.it

€€€

A LONG WALK
SENTIERO AZZURRO

Distance 16 km (10 miles) **Walking time** 4 hours **Terrain**
The route involves around 600 m (1900 ft) of elevation. Most
of the trail is not paved and some parts have hazardous terrain

The Sentiero Azzurro, or Blue Path, is one of the most beautiful (and deservedly popular) hikes in Italy. The route takes in each of the picturesque towns of the Cinque Terre, but the real joy is the undulating clifftop terrain that links them. The route starts in the town of Monterosso and finishes in Riomaggiore. The most popular section of the route – the

Via dell'Amore (p113), between Corniglia and Riomaggiore – was closed for nearly a decade up until 2023 for renovation, due to damage by dangerous landslides. This was caused in part by heavy foot traffic, so when walking ensure you stick to the path. Note that a ticket is required to access stretches of the route (www.card.parconazionale5terre.it).

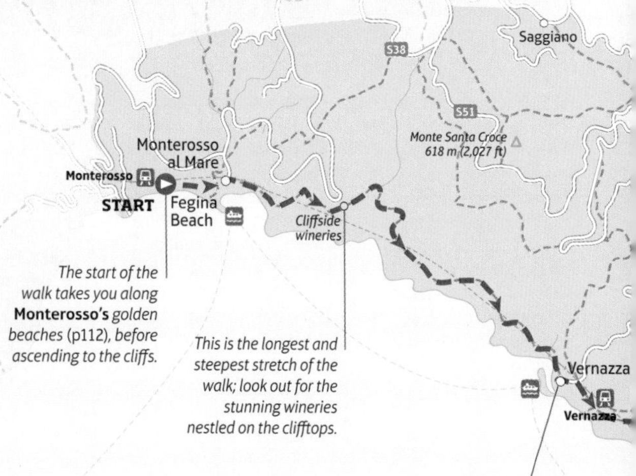

Saggiano

S38

S51

Monte Santa Croce
618 m (2,027 ft)

Monterosso
al Mare

Monterosso

START Fegina
Beach

Cliffside
wineries

Vernazza

Vernazza

The start of the walk takes you along **Monterosso's** *golden beaches (p112), before ascending to the cliffs.*

This is the longest and steepest stretch of the walk; look out for the stunning wineries nestled on the clifftops.

Take a well deserved break in the town of **Vernazza** *(p114), arguably the prettiest of the five villages, with its colourful houses squeezed at the foot of terraced vineyards.*

0 kilometres   20

0 miles   20

N
↑

← The Sentiero Azzurro, leading from Vernazza to Corniglia

↑ Delightful paved section of the Sentiero Azzurro, leading to the town of Manarola

Locator Map

RIVIERA DI LEVANTE

Sentiero Azzurro

Having refreshed in Vernazza, rejoin the path to Corniglia (the route is waymarked on the eastern edge of Vernazza).

Fontanella

Murro

S51

Case Fornacchi

Mediterranean flora

Look out for a range of Mediterranean flora on the route.

Case Pianca

Riviera di Levante

Porciana

Corniglia

🚌 **Corniglia**

Volastra

Groppo

S51

Poggio Leandro 405 m (1,328 ft)

*From the pretty village of **Corniglia** (p114), you can now join the beloved Via dell'Amore.*

Manarola

🏛️🚌 **Manarola**

S370

*At **Manarola** (p113), you can see the extensive cliff-side engineering designed to prevent future landslides.*

Riomaggiore

🏛️🚌

FINISH ⬜ Riomaggiore

*The Via dell'Amore ends in **Riomaggiore** (p114), with stunning sea views.*

> 💬 INSIDER TIP
> ## Way of Love
> Since the Via dell'Amore was reopened, visitor numbers have been limited and a walking slot must be booked online. Check *www.viadellamore.info* for more information on the route.

❸

LA SPEZIA

🅰 G5 🄵🄢 🚌 ℹ Piazza Europa 1; www.visitspezia.it

Once a trading centre for spices (*la spezia* means spice), the port of La Spezia transformed in the 13th century after a fortress was built here. It changed radically again in 1861 when a naval base was constructed. Today, traces of the past are tucked away amid the sprawling metropolis, home to an array of museums and churches.

① 🏛 Ⓜ

Museo Amedeo Lia

🏛 Via Prione 234 🕐 10am-6pm Tue-Sun 🚫 1 Jan, 15 Aug, 25 Dec 🌐 museolia.spezianet.it

This award-winning museum, opened in 1996, is based on the works donated by Amedeo Lia and his family. It is housed in a part of the monastery of the monks of San Francesco da Paola. The museum includes paintings and miniatures, medieval ivory, Limoges enamels, medals and numerous archaeological finds from the Mediterranean basin.

Paintings are the collection's most notable element, though: the 13th- and 14th-century paintings form one of Europe's finest private collections. Besides works by Paolo di Giovanni Fei, Sassetta and Lippo di Benivieni, there are two 16th-century highlights: a presumed *Self Portrait* (1520) by Pontormo and *Portrait of a Gentleman* (1510) by Titian.

📷 PICTURE PERFECT
Le Scalinate

The grand Le Scalinate staircase in La Spezia's historic centre offers a chance to snap a panorama of the city. Bordered by tropical plants, the steep stairs gradually reveal the gulf as you climb.

The 17th-century paintings by Caravaggio's followers are also significant, as are the Venetian views by Canaletto, Bellotto, Marieschi and Guardi. There are bronzes from the 16th and 17th centuries too.

---

② 🏛 Ⓜ

Museo Tecnico Navale della Spezia

🏛 Viale Amendola 1 🕐 8:30am-7:30pm daily 🚫 1 Jan, 15 Aug, 25 Dec 🌐 marina.difesa.it

The construction of the naval base from Genoa to La Spezia was undertaken by the Savoy government under Camillo Benso, Count of Cavour in 1861. The city inevitably expanded as a result, and from 1861 to 1881 the number of inhabitants tripled. Badly damaged by bombing in World War II, and again by German troops who occupied the site between 1943 and 1945, the base was meticulously reconstructed.

The predominant style of the structure is Neo-Classical. It also illustrates how the designer, Colonel Domenico Chiodo, responded to practical requirements: for instance, the workshops are located near the entrance for the workers'

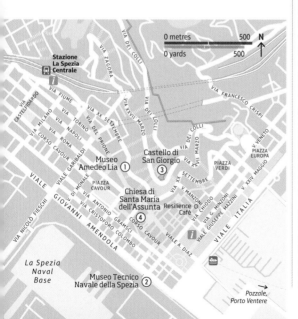

The Thaon de Revel Bridge set against La Spezia's iconic skyline

convenience, and the offices and warehouse are placed centrally. You can visit parts of the base, including the old workshops, sailmakers' yards, docks and the swing bridge.

The museum itself is one of Italy's oldest and most important naval museums. The core of its collection dates back to the 16th century, and was started by Emanuel Philibert of Savoy, who gathered mementoes from the Battle of Lepanto (1571). Models help illustrate the port's history; there is also a fine collection of anchors and a display of figureheads from old sailing ships.

↑ A wooden figurehead from the Museo Tecnico Navale della Spezia

③
Castello di San Giorgio

⌂ Via XXVII Marzo ☏ 0187 751 142 🕐 Hours vary, call ahead 🗓 1 Jan, 24 & 25 Dec

The oldest architectural vestige of centuries past, the Castello di San Giorgio occupies a commanding position overlooking the port with its Thaon de Revel suspension bridge . The imposing fortification was commissioned by the Fieschi family in the 13th century, though what is seen today dates from a 14th-century reconstruction, and from defence work carried out in the 17th century. The castle is now home to the **Museo Civico Archeologico Ubaldo Formentini**.

The archaeological museum was established in the 19th century to house finds discovered during excavation work carried out on the naval base. Some of these remarkable finds evidence the first human settlements in Lunigiana: coins and ceramics from the prehistoric, Etruscan and Roman eras are among the objects found near the ancient city of Luni (p130). Also notable are Palaeolithic finds from the Grotta dei Colombi, vast caves found on the island of Palmaria (p128). The most significant section of the museum is, however, the collection of statue-stelae. These sandstone sculptures, dating from the Bronze and Iron ages, depict women and warriers.

Museo Civico Archeologico Ubaldo Formentini

🚼♿👶⌂ Castello di San Giorgio, Via XXVII Marzo 🕐 Hours vary, check website 🗓 1 Jan, 24–26 Dec Ⓦ museo delcastello.spezianet.it

④
Chiesa di Santa Maria dell'Assunta

⌂ Piazza Beverini 🕐 8–10am & 11:30am–6pm daily

This 14th-century church has been modified more than once. Its appearance today, with its black-and-white façade, owes much to reconstruction after the war. It houses the *Coronation of the Virgin*, a glazed terracotta relief by artist Andrea Della Robbia and Luca Cambiaso's masterful 16th-century painting, *Martyrdom of St Bartholomew.*

4

SARZANA

G5 Province of La Spezia FS Piazza San Giorgio; 0187 305 551; www.comune.sarzana.sp.it

This lively agricultural and commercial town has a tumultuous past; it was held first by Pisa, then Florence and the Republic of Genoa. A sophisticated town, Sarzana has a splendid historic centre and brings purveyors from all over Italy for its famous antiques market, which lasts for two weeks in August.

①

Church of Sant'Andrea

Via Mazzini 23/25

This Romanesque parish church is one of the oldest buildings in Sarzana, dating back to the 10th century. It was substantially enlarged in the 16th century, when an unusual door decorated with caryatids was added. Above the door is an eight-pointed star and a shield, the symbol of Sarzana. The church's square bell tower is characteristic of other Romanesque church towers in the region, but most of its original features have been lost due to centuries of renovation, and the stone façade has lost its character. It's worth venturing inside, however, where you'll find striking altarpieces and an 18th-century organ.

②

Cittadella

Piazza Cittadella 19038

This imposing fortress, also known as the Fortezza Firmafede, was built by Lorenzo the Magnificent, the powerful Medici ruler of Florence from 1488 to 92. It is built on a rectangular plan with six round towers and a moat. The 16th-century walls were constructed by the Genoese. During World War II, it was used to hold prisoners of war.

③

Cathedral of Santa Maria Assunta

Via Nicolò V 2 0187 620 017 8am-noon & 3-6:30pm Mon-Sat, 11-11:30am & 3-3:30pm Sun

The construction of the cathedral of Santa Maria Assunta, begun in 1204 after the transfer of the bishopric from Luni to Sarzana, was completed in the 15th century and modified in the 17th century. The 14th-century door, the finely carved marble rose window and the bell tower are all enchanting. Inside, there are two intricate

DEFENDING THE TOWN

North of Sarzana, the Fortress of Sarzanello commands a strategic position over lower Lunigiana. Built for Castruccio Castracani, a lord of Lucca, in around 1322, the fort is built on a triangular plan and has three cylindrical corner towers. Access is via a bridge which straddles a deep moat.

↓ The town of Sarzana

② Sarzanello

③

①

④

15th-century marble altarpieces by Leonardo Riccomanni. *The Cross of Maestro Guglielmo*, the work of a Tuscan artist, dated 1138, can be seen in the Cathedral. It became a prototype for the crucifixes that were painted in Tuscany and Umbria in the following two centuries.

---

④
Porta Romana

📍 Via Mazzini, 19038

Found just south of Sarzana's Old Town, Porta Romana is a richly decorated Roman city wall. The wall features a monumental gate with a single large arch, constructed in marble. Above the arch there is a small shrine containing a statue of the Virgin Mary in prayer. Through the gate, in a small vault, lies the city coat of arms, featuring a half moon and Sarzana's symbol, the eight-point star. The wall leads through to Sarzana's delightful cobbled streets; heading out of the city, it points travellers in the direction of Rome.

EAT

Antica Osteria Tre Archi
Serving traditional fare since 1984, this *osteria* also offers set menus.

📍 Via Sotto Gli Uffizi 18
🌐 anticaosteria trearchi.it

€€€

Il Viandante
Popular with local walkers, this family restaurant serves homemade cuisine.

📍 Via Rossi 3/7
📞 0187 305 868

€€€

Il Panìgo
Enjoy hearty dishes and wine in a bustling dining room.

📍 Via Cisa 131
🌐 ristoranteilpanigo.it

€€€

↑ Dining al fresco in Sarzana's main square, Piazza Matteotti

EXPERIENCE MORE

⑤
Bogliasco

🅰E4 🏠Genoa 🚉🚌
ℹ️ Via Aurelia 106; www.
prolocobogliasco.it

On the aptly named Golfo di Paradiso east of Genoa, Bogliasco is an elegant residential and tourist town with a few small beaches. It retains the look of a traditional fishing village with painted houses arranged prettily around the mouth of the River Bogliasco (crossed by a medieval bridge known as the Ponte Romano).

The town is dominated by the 1,000-year-old Castello, a defensive tower built by the Republic of Genoa. To the west, high up on a cliff, is the 18th-century parish church, with a terrace of black and white pebbles. The 15th-century Oratory of Santa Chiara is also noteworthy, and has several highly ornate, traditional processional crosses, among them one by Maragliano.

⑥
Camogli

🅰E4 🏠Genoa 🚉🚌
ℹ️ Via XX Settembre 33;
www.camogliturismo.it

An old fishing and seafaring village on the Golfo di Paradiso, Camogli is named after the *moglie* (women) who ran the town while their husbands were at sea. The village centre has tall, narrow houses crowded around the harbour and along the maze of alleys and steps behind.

A small promontory, known as the "Isola" (island), is home to the Basilica di Santa Maria Assunta, founded in the 12th century, but much modified. It has a Neo-Classical façade and a 17th-century pebbled courtyard. The richly decorated interior features a frescoed vault in the central nave by Francesco Semino and Nicolò Barabino, and the high altar has an 18th-century sculpture of the Virgin Mary by Bernardo Schiaffino. On a cliff

overlooking the sea stands the medieval Castel Dragone.

At the end of the seafront is the **Museo Marinaro Gio Bono Ferrari**. This museum documents a prosperous time in Camogli's history: namely, the 18th and 19th centuries, when Camogli supplied a fleet of some 3,000 merchant ships under contract to the major European states – they even fought with Napoleon. The museum also has ship models, paintings of ships (which served as ex-votos) and navigational instruments. The cloister next to the sanctuary of

---

🔍 HIDDEN GEM
Fireworks in Camogli

During the Festa di San Fortunato in October, a spectacular fireworks display takes place on the beach followed by the burning of *falò* (huge sculptures made of scrap material).

← Colourful buildings overlooking the beach in Camogli

Nostra Signora del Boschetto, just outside Camogli, also has sailors' ex-votos on display.

Museo Marinaro Gio Bono Ferrari

 🏛 Via GB Ferrari 41 📞 0185 729 049 🕐 9am-noon Tue-Sun

❼ Santa Margherita Ligure

🗺 E4 🚊 Genoa 🚆🚌 ℹ️ Piazza Vittorio Veneto; www.livesanta.it

Built along an inlet on the Golfo del Tigullio, Santa Margherita Ligure is a lively resort named after the lavish Rococo church of Santa Margherita d'Antiochia.

The town emerged in its own right only in the 19th century, when it was created out of the two villages of Pescino and Corte. It soon became a popular destination among the holidaying elite and is home to a beautiful harbour with grand hotels.

The hill between the two old villages has been transformed into the public Parco di Villa Durazzo. This 16th-century villa has original furnishings and a fine art collection. Its Italian-style garden offers lovely views of the city and the sea.

❽ Torriglia

🗺 E4 🚊 Genoa 🚆🚌 ℹ️ Ente Parco d'Antola: Via Nostra Signora della Provvidenza 3; www.parcoantola.it

This small holiday resort is set in the forested Antola mountains. In the Roman period it was a significant commercial centre, located at an important crossroads on the main route between Genoa and Emilia-Romagna.

The town overlooks the imposing ruins of a medieval castle. Built by the Malaspina family, it was later occupied by the Fieschi family and, from the second half of the 16th century, by the Doria dynasty.

Two pleasant trips can be made from Torriglia. The first is to Pentema, about 6 km (4 miles) north of the town along a winding road.

STAY

Hotel Cenobio dei Dogi

With sea views, this four-star hotel has a private beach area and swimming pool.

🗺 E4 🏛 Via Nicolò Cuneo 34, Camogli 🌐 cenobio.it

€€€

Villa Rosmarino

Nestled on the hillside above Camogli, this modern boutique hotel features grounds shaded by camellias, roses and pomegranate trees.

🗺 E4 🏛 Via Enrico Figari, Camogli 🌐 villarosmarino.com

€€€

Locanda I Tre Merli

Overlooking the marina, this hotel has luxurious rooms and a wellness centre on site.

🗺 E4 🏛 Via dello Scalo 5, Camogli 🌐 locandaitremerli.com

€€€

Having crossed the stunning landscape of hills and mountains covered in dense forest, walkers will reach one of the loveliest villages inland from the Riviera di Levante.

Some 8 km (5 miles) east of Torriglia is the wonderfully peaceful Lago del Brugneto, an artificial basin created as a reservoir for Genoa. The lake lies within the Parco Regionale dell'Antola and is entirely surrounded by hills and mountains. A scenic walking trail snakes around the shores of the lake: some 13 km (8 miles) long, the walk takes about six hours to complete.

⑨ Rapallo

🅰E4 🚊Genoa 🚇🚌
ℹPiazza IV Novembre;
www.prolocorapallo.org

Rapallo is perhaps the best-known resort along Riviera di Levante. It has a large marina, swimming pool and an 18-hole golf course.

In the 19th century, the warm climate was a big attraction for aristocrats, who visited the Art Nouveau cafés and hotels lining Lungomare Vittorio Veneto. Max Beerbohm (1872–1956), the English critic, was a resident for many years.

In the centre, the streets Via Venezia, Via Mazzini and Via Marsala define the medieval "*borgo murato*" (walled village), so-named because of the way the buildings are closely packed together. The centre is also home to historic monuments such as the parish church of Santo Stefano (17th century), the 15th-century civic tower, a 16th-century Castello and the medieval Ponte di Annibale (Hannibal's Bridge). The Castello, built on a cliff to defend the settlement against pirate raids, can be reached from Piazza Pastene. There is also a funicular ride up to the 16th-century Santuario di Montallegro, offering coastal views.

The **Museo del Merletto**, housed in Rapallo's lavish Villa Tigullio, is a museum of lace with more than 1,400 pieces from the 16th to 19th centuries. Among these are lace for clothing, furnishing, and several 18th–19th century pillows. There is also a collection of lace designs. Just east of Rapallo, the small resort of Zoagli has the feel of a fishing village.

Museo del Merletto

⊗ 🅰Villa Tigullio, Parco Casale 📞0185 633 05 🕐2:30–4:30pm Tue–Sun (from 10am Sat & Sun)

⑩ Santo Stefano d'Aveto

🅰F4 🚊Genoa 🚌 ℹPiazza del Popolo 6; www.comune. santostefanodaveto.ge.it

Situated in an Alpine-looking hollow, dominated by Monte Maggiorasca, Santo Stefano d'Aveto is a delightful mountain village. Visitors can stroll around the pretty, historic centre, with its winding alleys and small squares. It is also a popular base for cross-country skiing in winter.

Near the town are the imposing ruins of Castello Malaspina, built by the local nobles in the 12th century, and subsequently passed to the Fieschi and Doria families.

The Val d'Aveto was formed by the Aveto torrent, which carves out an upland plain southwest of the village, where pastures are enclosed by mountains covered in forests of silver fir, Norway spruce, and beech and ash

← The funicular ride provides breathtaking views of Rapallo

← Decorated interior of Chiavari's Nostra Signora dell'Orto cathedral, and *(inset)* its Neo-Classical façade with Corinthian columns

trees. Much of this is now part of the Parco Naturale Regionale dell'Aveto.

From Santo Stefano, visitors can reach Monte Aiona – the tallest peak in the Parco Naturale at 1,700 m (5,581 ft) – along trails that reveal the beauty of this unspoiled area. Note that the western slopes form part of the Riserva Naturale delle Agoraie and are closed to public.

Also near the village is the forest of Le Lame, with its marshes and small lakes of glacial origin. Some 2,500-year-old fir trunks are preserved in the ice-cold water and can be seen lying at the bottom of Lago degli Abeti.

---

⑪ Chiavari

⌂F4 ⌂Genoa 🚉🚌
🛈 Via della Cittadella; www.chiavariturismo.it

Chiavari stands on an alluvial plain on the eastern shores of the Golfo del Tigullio and on the west bank of the Entella torrent. Called Clavarium ("key to the valleys") by the Romans, the town was once known for its old crafts, particularly shipbuilding, chair-making and macramé. Nowadays, tourism is the most important source of income.

The ruins of a necropolis, dating from the 8th–7th centuries BCE, now held in the local archaeological museum, demonstrate that the area was inhabited by the Liguri Tigullio people in the pre-Roman era. The fortified town of Chiavari dates from 1178, when the Genoese expanded into the Riviera di Levante in the struggle to counter the power of the Fieschi family.

At the heart of Chiavari is Piazza Mazzini, around which the arcaded streets of the old city are laid out. One of these, Via dei Martiri della Liberazione, is a straight alleyway known as a *"carruggiu dritu"*, which was occupied by the bourgeoisie from the 14th century.

The cathedral, Nostra Signora dell'Orto, has 17th-century origins but was rebuilt in the 19th–20th centuries. Inside, the interior is decorated with gilded stucco and marble inlay, displaying works by Orazio de Ferrari and Anton Maria Maragliano. The 12th-century parish church of San Giovanni Battista was rebuilt in 1624. On the outskirts, at Bacezza, is the 15th-century Santuario della Madonna delle Grazie, which offers stunning views stretching from Portofino to Sestri Levante. Inside is a 16th-century cycle of frescoes by Teramo Piaggio and Luca Cambiaso.

---

⑫ ⓂS Abbazia di Sant'Andrea di Borzone

⌂F4 ⌂Località Borzone, 63, Borzonasca 🚉Chiavari
🚌 📞0185 340 056 ⏰8am–6:30pm daily; call ahead for tours

This lovely abbey can be reached along a winding road that runs eastwards from the centre of Borzonasca, an inland town that is 16 km (10 miles) from Chiavari.

Standing in isolation, Sant'Andrea is one of the oldest Benedictine settlements in Italy. It was founded in the 12th century by the monks of San Colombano in Bobbio (in Emilia-Romagna) and donated in 1184 to the Benedictines of Marseille, who reclaimed the land and used it for cultivation.

The monks undertook a programme of terracing and irrigation. Even today, despite the fact that the woods have begun to encroach, the remains of dry stone walls can still be seen along the paths. The abbey was rebuilt in the 13th century, at the request of the Fieschi counts, but has managed to retain its original Romanesque look.

The church, with a square bell tower, is built of brick and stone. It has a single nave and a semicircular apse, and a cornice of terracotta arches. Several cloister columns survive from the old monastery. In the presbytery there is a polyptych dating from 1484, by an unknown Genoese artist, and a slate tabernacle from 1513.

13

Bonassola

⚑F5 ⬠La Spezia 🚌 **ℹ Via Fratelli Rezzano; www.prolocobonassola.it**

Built around a cove, Bonassola was selected by the Genoese in the 13th century as the site for a defensive naval base. Now the town has no marina, but it is not difficult to land small boats here. It has a wide pebbled beach and a sea bed that is varied and suited to dives of medium difficulty.

The town is home to the 16th-century parish church of Santa Caterina, which features rich Baroque decoration and numerous ex-votos – evidence of the seafaring lives of the inhabitants. To the west of the village, the church of Madonna della Punta, perched on a cliff jutting out over the sea, is a popular spot for sunset views.

Several old villages in the vicinity are worth exploring on foot. A 9-km (6-mile) path, following a route through vineyards and olive groves, takes walkers to Montaretto, known for its production of good white wine.

14

Lavagna

⚑F4 🚌 **ℹ Piazza della Libertà 47; www.comune. lavagna.ge.it**

This coastal town lies across the Entella from Chiavari, to which it is linked by several bridges, including the fine medieval Ponte della Maddalena.

In the Middle Ages this town was a stronghold of the local Fieschi counts. Historically, its prosperity has been due to the local slate quarries. Today, the town depends more on its beach and marina, which has more than 1,500 yachts.

Historic monuments include the 10th-century church of Santo Stefano, which was rebuilt in 1653 when a Baroque staircase and asymmetrical

---

LIGURIAN SLATE

From the black stripes of San Salvatore dei Fieschi to the roofs of numerous private houses, slate is a characteristic element of many buildings in the Riviera di Levante. Today, it is still quarried in the hinterland behind Chiavari (not far, in fact, from the town of Lavagna, which means "blackboard" in Italian).

---

bell towers were added; the grand 17th-century Palazzo Franzone, now the town hall; and the church of Santa Giulia di Centaura, reached along a scenic road from Viale Mazzini and with panoramic views along the coast.

A 30-minute walk inland from Lavagna is the village of San Salvatore di Cogorno, from where visitors can reach the **Basilica di San Salvatore dei Fieschi**, one of the most important Romanesque-Gothic monuments in Liguria. It was commissioned in 1245 by Ottobono Fieschi, the future Pope Adrian V and nephew of Pope Innocent IV (another Fieschi), who made it a basilica in 1252. The building is perched on the top of

---

a hill covered in olive groves, and surrounded by ancient buildings, among them the ruined 13th-century Palazzo dei Conti Fieschi.

The church is dominated by a powerful square tower which rises over the crossing. It has cornices of blind arches and four-mullioned windows, and is crowned with a tall spire with four pinnacles. The upper façade is decorated with alternating bands of marble and slate, and a large rose window. The marble and slate striped bands are repeated inside the rather austere interior, and slate is used elsewhere, too, in the form of tiles in the transept and presbytery.

Basilica di San Salvatore dei Fieschi

⬠ Piazza Innocenzo IV, San Salvatore di Cogorno
📞 0185 380245 🕐 Daily

15

Sestri Levante

⚑F5 ⬠Genoa 🚌 **ℹ Corso Colombo 50; open 9am–1pm & 2–5pm daily; www.sestri-levante.net**

At the far western point of the Golfo del Tigullio, Sestri Levante is one of the liveliest resorts on the coast. It clusters around a rocky peninsula

↑ The monumental structure of the Basilica di San Salvatore dei Fieschi in Lavagna

← Boats moored alongside the pastel houses in Baia del Silenzio, Sestri Levante

known as the "Isola" and is home to interesting monuments: the early 17th-century Basilica di Santa Maria di Nazareth by Giovanni Battista Carlone; the 17th-century Palazzo Durazzo Pallavicini, which is now the town hall; and the lovely 12th-century Romanesque church of San Nicolò dell'Isola.

At the tip of the peninsula is the Grand Hotel dei Castelli, built in the 1920s on the site of an old castle. The hotel has a magnificent park overlooking two bays: the sandy Baia delle Favole, named after Hans Christian Andersen, who stayed here in 1833 (*favole* means fairy tales); and the smaller and quieter Baia del Silenzio, framed by multicoloured houses and dotted with fishing boats. The hotel's grounds also have a tower where Marconi carried out some of his radio experiments in 1934.

Back in the old town, the **Galleria Rizzi** showcases paintings, sculptures, ceramics and furniture collected by the local Rizzi family. The paintings include works by Giovanni Andrea de Ferrari and Alessandro Magnasco.

Galleria Rizzi
⊛ 🏠 Via dei Cappuccini 8
📞 0185 413 00 🕐 Apr-Oct: 10am-1pm Sun; May-Sep: 4-7pm Wed; mid-Jun-Sep: 9:30-11:30pm Fri & Sat

16

Varese Ligure

🅰F4 🚉 La Spezia 🚌 From Sestri Levante 🛈 Via Portici 19; www.comune. vareseligure.sp.it

This inland summer resort was an important market town for centuries. Over time, the town acquired the rural role it has today and agriculture became the main trade in this region.

Varese Ligure was a possession of the Fieschi family, who obtained it in fief from Emperor Frederick I in 1161. They built the splendid 15th-century castle in a piazza, which was once a market square called Borgo Rotondo. A ring of multicoloured shops and houses were built around this piazza and the façades are supported by arches and porticoes. The nearby Borgo Nuovo features aristocratic palazzi dating from the 16th to 19th centuries.

The River Crovana, crossed by a medieval bridge, is one of the tributaries of the Vara, whose valley, the Val di Vara, extends for more than 60 km (37 miles) and has a varied landscape. The upper reaches of the river flow through wonderful mountain scenery, interspersed by meadows where cows and horses graze. Elsewhere there are scenic stretches where the river is confined between rocks. Towards the coast, the valley widens and the river flows through the Parco Naturale Regionale di Montemarcello-Magra (*p133*).

DRINK

Capocotta
Enjoy innovative tapas dishes alongside a selection of refined wines at this lounge bar.

🅰F5 🏠 Vico Macelli 8, Sestri Levante
📞 0185 189 8193

Sky Bar Zeus
Set in Hotel Vis à Vis, this rooftop bar offers incredible views over Sestri Levante.

🅰F5 🏠 Via della Chiusa 28, Sestri Levante
📞 0185 42 661

Millelire
This dynamic bar features a wide array of drinks and hosts live music shows.

🅰F5 🏠 Via XXV Aprile, 153, Sestri Levante
🌐 ivinaccieri.com

STAY

Villa Valentina B&B

At this B&B, guests can dine under a pergola.

🅰F5 🏠Pié Di Legnaro 1, Levanto 🌐villa valentina5terre.com

€€€

Hotel Palazzo Vannoni

A three-star property housed in a palazzo.

🅰F5 🏠Via Guglielmo Marconi 4, Levanto 🌐hotelpalazzovannoni.it

€€€

Grand Hotel

This five-star hotel is set in a former 17th-century monastery,.

🅰G5 🏠Via Giuseppe Garibaldi 5, Portovenere 🌐portovenereregrand.com

€€€

⓱ Palmaria, Tino and Tinetto

🅰G6 🏠La Spezia 🚢From La Spezia or Portovenere for Isola Palmaria 🅸IAT Portovenere; www. barcaioliportovenere.com

Liguria's only archipelago once formed part of the headland of Portovenere. The largest island, Isola Palmaria, is divided from the mainland by just a narrow channel. It is covered in dense vegetation on one side, and has steep cliffs and caves on the other. In the past, Portor marble, a valuable black stone used in some buildings in Portovenere, was quarried here, which has partially disfigured the island.

The much smaller islands of Tino and Tinetto lie in a military zone. Tino features a lighthouse that guides ships into the gulf. Access to the island is allowed only on 13 September, for the Festa di San Venerio. There is a ruined 11th-century abbey, built on the site of a chapel where a hermit saint lived in solitude.

Tinetto is an inhospitable rock, but the rich diversity of the seabed make this a popular diving area. The island is also home to the ruins of two 5th-century religious structures, confirming the earliest known Christian presence in the area.

⓲ Portovenere

🅰G5 🏠La Spezia 🚆🚌 🅸Piazza Bastreri 7; www.portovenere.com

Lying at the base of a rocky cliff, Portovenere resembles a fortified fishing village with its brightly painted houses by the harbour. Further inland is a maze of narrow alleys and vaulted staircases, populated by the town's numerous cats.

At the tip of the headland is the 13th-century church of San Pietro. Built in honour of the patron saint of fishers, it retains elements dating from the 6th century and has a small Romanesque loggia.

The church of San Lorenzo is a short walk up an alley from the harbour. This 12th-century Romanesque church, reworked in the Gothic and Renaissance eras, has rustic interiors.

Further up the alley, visitors will reach the 16th-century **Castello Doria**. Built by the

→

The striped exterior of the church of Sant'Andrea with a stunning rose window

Genoese, this grand example of military architecture offers fantastic views and is linked to the town by a line of walls with square towers.

Le Grazie, along the winding route north from Portovenere to La Spezia, is another place of great beauty. Monte Muzzerone nearby is hugely popular among free-climbers. The village is home to the 15th-century church of Santa Maria delle Grazie and the 16th-century monastery of the Olivetans. By the inlet of Varignano, close by, is a ruined Roman villa, dating from the 2nd–1st century BCE, with a mosaic pavement and a small museum, known as the **Antiquarium del Varignano**.

Castello Doria

⊛ 🕘10am-6pm daily 🌐 parco naturaleportovenere.it

Antiquarium del Varignano

🏠 Le Grazie 📞 0187 790 307 🕘 8:30am-6:30pm Tue-Sun (Sun: to 1:30pm)

19

Levanto

🅰 F5 🏠 La Spezia 🚆 ℹ Piazza Cavour 1; www. comune.levanto.sp.it

Over the years, Levanto has been a centre for trade and agriculture. It has a long and lovely beach that attracts holidaymakers. The small town is divided into Borgo Antico (the medieval district around the church of Sant'Andrea and the hill of San Giacomo), and the Borgo

←

Church of San Pietro perched on a headland overlooking the Ligurian Sea, Portovenere

Nuovo (which developed in the 15th century on the nearby plain). In the medieval district is the 13th-century Loggia del Comune, the Casa Restani, with a 13th–14th-century portico, a privately owned castle and a stretch of the old town walls, dating from 1265.

The principal monument is the parish church of Sant' Andrea, a beautiful example of Ligurian Gothic. Its façade is striped with white marble and local serpentine (a softish green stone), with a finely carved rose window. The columns in the nave also show hints of serpentine stone. An array of artworks can be found including two canvases from a polyptych by Carlo Braccesco depicting *Saints Augustine and Jerome* and *Saints Blaise and Pantaleon*. In the former oratory of the church is a **Museo Permanente della Cultura Materiale**, which reconstructs various aspects of the rural and seafaring life of the Riviera di Levante.

Among vestiges of Levanto's more recent past are several

INSIDER TIP
Pedal Power

Hire a bike in Levanto and cycle along an old railway line to Framura, passing the little village of Bonassola. The paved coastal road snakes past several tunnels and offers lovely sea views.

---

palazzi dating from the 17th and 18th centuries, when many Genoese noble families built their summer residences here: Palazzo Vannoni, facing on to Piazza Cavour, is the most prominent of these.

Museo Permanente della Cultura Materiale

🏠 Via San Nicolò 1 📞 0187 817 776 🕘 Jun-Sep: 9:20am-11:30pm Fri-Sun & public hols

---

20

Campiglia

🅰 G5 🏠 La Spezia 🚆🚌 From La Spezia ℹ IAT Cinque Terre; www.tramontidi campiglia.it

Founded in the Middle Ages, this rural village occupies a precipitous position near the coast and is only a short distance from La Spezia.

Campiglia was built on an old mule road along the ridge between Portovenere and Levanto, and it is still a great starting point for walks. The most beautiful, and hardest, walk is along CAI (Italian Alpine Club) path no. 11. This track takes visitors through the spectacular terrain of the Tramonti, a continuation of the Cinque Terre with terraces of vines, before a steep flight of 2,000 steps descends down as far as the small beach of Punta del Persico: the landscape open to the sea is genuinely breathtaking.

㉑
Luni

⌂ G5 ⌂ La Spezia ▭ ℹ Via Appia 9, Ortonovo; 0187 668 11; Site and museum: open 8:30am-2pm Tue-Sun (Sat: to 7:30pm), closed 25 Dec, 1 Jan, 1 May

The Roman colony of Portus Lunae was founded in 177 BCE in an effort to counter the native Ligurians. Its role as an important port grew as Luni became a major channel for the shipping of marble from the nearby Apuan Alps (known as Luni marble) to all corners of the Roman empire.

Luni's prosperity faltered during the early centuries of the Middle Ages due to the gradual decrease of the marble trade, with a full-blown decline accompanying the silting-up of the harbour. The coast is now 2 km (1 mile)

Did You Know?

Luni's white wine has hints of wild flowers, herbs and honey, making it the perfect pairing for pesto.

away. In 1204, the bishopric was moved to nearby Sarzana, and soon all that was left of Luni was its name, which had also given the surrounding area its title, the Lunigiana.

The archaeological site at Luni is the most important one in northern Italy. Surrounded by walls, the city was built to a perfectly regular layout, with the public buildings equally neatly placed. A great temple and several prestigious houses stood near the huge, marble-paved Forum. Nearby was the Capitolium, a temple dedicated to Jove, Juno and Minerva, encircled by a marble-edged basin, with a flight of steps in front. Remains of these buildings are still visible.

Nearby was the Casa dei Mosaici, which had an atrium in Corinthian style surrounded by rooms with 3rd–4th-century CE mosaics; some of these still survive. The Casa degli Affreschi, built around a garden, had rooms with fine floors and frescoes. Inside the walls there are also the ruins of the Early Christian basilica of Santa Maria Assunta, including the remains of three early Romanesque apses.

Outside the walls is the amphitheatre, which was built in the Antonine era (1st–2nd century CE) and was the scene

of violent gladiatorial fights. The lower section of stepped seats, as well as part of a covered portico, survives. The complex system of steps and corridors that led to the seating is still visible.

On the site of the Forum is an archaeological museum, with displays of Imperial-era marble statues, busts, fragments of frescoes, jewellery, tools, stamps and ceramics.

㉒
Ameglia

⌂ G5 ⌂ La Spezia ▤ Sarzana, Santo Stefano Magra ▭ ℹ Piazza Francesco Sforza; www. comune.ameglia.sp.it

Close to the mouth of the River Magra, Ameglia still has the look of a hill town. Tall houses are packed together around a hilltop where a castle once stood. Its ruins include a round tower and parts of the original walls. The main part of the castle was replaced in the Renaissance period by the Palazzo del Podestà, later the Palazzo Comunale (town hall).

From the summit, alleys extend in concentric circles, broken up by small squares, several of which have a view

An amphitheatre at Luni, and (inset) a mosaic from the ancient Roman site

of the Carrara marble mountains. The lovely piazza in front of the church of Santi Vincenzo e Anastasio offers views over the lower Lunigiana and the Apuan Alps.

㉓
Bocca di Magra

🗺 G6 🚉 La Spezia 🚆 Sarzana, Santo Stefano Magra 🚌 ℹ️ Via Fabbricotti; 0187 608 037

Originally a fishing village at the mouth (bocca) of the River Magra, this resort manages to hold onto its heritage. In addition to numerous holiday homes, there is a small beach, a spa and a marina.

The coast here is very different from that of the Cinque Terre and the Golfo della Spezia. It is near here that the low-lying, sandy stretch, known as the Versilia coast, begins.

The appeal of Bocca di Magra, which stems largely from its combined seaside and riverside location, was not lost on writers, poets and other demanding holiday-makers, who were attracted to Bocca in the first half of the 20th century, just as they were to other towns in the area.

Nearby are the remains of a Roman villa dating from the 1st century CE. It is built on sloping terraces on the cliff, in a panoramic position above the mouth of the river.

㉔
Castelnuovo di Magra

🗺 G5 🚉 La Spezia 🚆 Sarzana, Santo Stefano Magra 🚌 ℹ️ Via Aurelia 141; 0187 693 334

It seems probable that the origins of this inland town coincided with the decline of nearby Luni and the abandonment of the port by its inhabitants.

Castelnuovo, built on a hilltop in view of the mouth of the River Magra, is spread out attractively along a ridge, with the church at one end and the bishop's palace (a 13th-century castle) at the other. Via Dante links the two landmarks and is lined with handsome palazzi. Sections of the old town walls and two 15th-century towers are still visible.

The church at one end of Via Dante is Santa Maria Maddalena, built in the late 16th century but with a 19th-century façade. The marble columns inside are thought to have come from Santa Maria Assunta at Luni. Inside is a Calvary by Brueghel the Younger.

Between Castelnuovo and Luni, up a very winding road, is Nicola, a pretty medieval hilltop village centred around the church of Santi Filippo e Giacomo.

> **The appeal of Bocca di Magra, which stems largely from its combined seaside and riverside location, was not lost on writers, poets and other demanding holidaymakers.**

Lerici's harbour, with the imposing Castello in the background ↑

25

San Terenzo

🅰G5 🚇La Spezia 🚆La Spezia 🚌 ℹ️Via Gozzano; 345 112 7027

San Terenzo lies on the northern side of the Golfo della Spezia, overlooking the pretty bay of Lerici. A small group of fishers' houses once clustered along the shore of this village, which was a favourite among certain 19th-century poets, including Percy Bysshe Shelley. Casa Magni, the last home Shelley shared with his wife Mary, is located nearby.

Sights to visit include a castle on a rocky promontory nearby; the church of Santa Maria Assunta; and Villa Marigola, which has lovely gardens. To offset the stark effects of mass tourism, it's best to arrive by train.

26

Lerici

🅰G5 🚇La Spezia 🚆La Spezia 🚌 ℹ️Loc. Venere Azzurra; 51 147 2959

In the Middle Ages, Lerici was a major port, and enjoyed both commercial and strategic importance.

Today, it is a popular tourist town, but one that retains a working community with a strong identity.

The old centre is dominated by the **Castello**, the most important example of military architecture in the region. Built by the Pisans in the 13th century to counter a Genoese fort at Portovenere, it was taken by Genoa shortly afterwards, and was enlarged in the 15th century. It is still in a remarkably good state, with a pentagonal tower and massive walls. There is an archaeological museum inside.

Below the castle is the lovely and sandy Baia di Maralunga, which is good for a swim.

Castello and Museo
⊘ 🏠Piazza San Giorgio
📞0187 969 042 🕐10am–1pm & 4–6pm Tue–Sun (Sat & Sun: to 9pm)

27

Montemarcello

🅰G6 🚇La Spezia 🚆La Spezia 🚌

This town on the eastern fringes of the Golfo della Spezia offers fantastic views, both west towards the gulf and east towards the Versilia coast. Montemarcello does not share the structure common to hilltowns. Lacking the traditional concentric

---

THE GULF OF POETS

In 1919, Italian playwright Sem Benelli described the Gulf of Lerici as the "Gulf of Poets" – a fitting tribute to the literary figures who arrived here in the 19th and 20th centuries. This beautiful gulf has fascinated many artists and intellectuals, from Percy Bysshe Shelley to Virginia Woolf. As a result, the Parco Culturale Golfo dei Poeti was established, which remains a cultural hub and a source of inspiration for local artists today.

arrangement, it is instead laid out on a square network, echoing the layout of the original Roman *castrum* (military camp). The houses in the oldest part, still partially enclosed by the remains of the town walls, are painted in the bright colours usually seen in coastal towns – an anomaly in a mountain village. The street layout and the architectural style of the houses give this town an unusual atmosphere, more akin to an holiday resort than a rural village. Today, it is a haven for Italian artists, which has partly saved the town from major redevelopment.

The landscape around the town is delightful: this is the southern tract of the **Parco Naturale Regionale di Montemarcello-Magra**, Liguria's only river park, which offers great opportunities for walks, with several marked hiking trails. The park extends from the summit of the eastern headland of the Golfo della Spezia as far as the plain of the River Magra. In the southern stretches, near Bocca di Magra, the vegetation and the wildlife are typically Mediterranean, while in the north of the park there are fields and wetlands.

Parco Naturale Regionale di Montemarcello-Magra
🏠 Via Paci Agostino 2, Sarzana Ⓦparcomagra.it

28

Fiascherino and Tellaro

🅰G6 🏠La Spezia 🇫🇸La Spezia 🚌 ℹLerici; www.terredilunigiana.com

These two pretty fishing villages of painted houses lie next to each other, just south of Lerici. Both face small bays, with verdant hills behind.

Tiny Fiascherino has a lovely beach, and the cliffs conceal enchanting coves accessible only by boat. The writer DH Lawrence lived in the village in 1913–14.

Thanks to its position on the cliffs high above the sea, medieval Tellaro has preserved its original features almost intact, though the instability of the rock itself has caused some damage. The oldest part is built on a promontory that marks the furthermost limit of the Riviera di Levante: the tall houses here had to be built on different levels in order to accommodate the undulating terrain. The village's extremely narrow streets are linked by flights of steps and tunnels. The Baroque church of San Giorgio overlooks the sea, while the Oratory of In Selàa has a lovely courtyard, which also faces the tranquil coastal water.

EAT

Il Frantoio
This restaurant offers fish and seafood dishes.

🅰G5 🏠Via Cavour 21 Ⓦristoranteilfrantoio lerici.it

€€€

Bontà Nascoste
Tuck into fish and meat dishes here.

🅰G5 🏠Via Cavour 52, Lerici Ⓦbontanascoste.it

€€€

Locanda Miranda
Enjoy innovative dishes at this *locanda* (inn).

🅰G6 🏠Via Fiascherino 92, Tellaro
☎0187968130

€€€

→

Tellaro's tall, brightly painted houses lining its picturesque harbour

THE RIVIERA DI PONENTE

With the capital city of Genoa at one end and Ventimiglia, on the border with France, at the other, the Riviera di Ponente extends for around 150 km (93 miles) in the west of Liguria. At the prehistoric site of Balzi Rossi, Palaeolithic utensils and burial tombs have been found, yielding fascinating evidence of the region's earliest inhabitants. Traces of the Romans can be seen both on the coast and in the interior, particularly at the five Roman bridges in the Parco del Finalese or at the excavations of Albintimilium in ancient Ventimiglia. As the area's numerous medieval villages attest, the Ponente has had a long and rich human history.

Just like the Riviera di Levante, the Riviera di Ponente became a favourite holiday destination among the European aristocracy from the late 19th century. Hotels and Art Nouveau villas are still in evidence almost everywhere, hangovers from this time of luxury holidaymaking.

The two provincial capitals on the Riviera di Ponente are Savona and Imperia. Sanremo, with its grand Art Nouveau architecture, is the main holiday resort. New developments now dominate the coast closest to Genoa, but away from here the region is so green and lush that it is divided into the Riviera delle Palme ("of palm trees") and the Riviera dei Fiori ("of flowers").

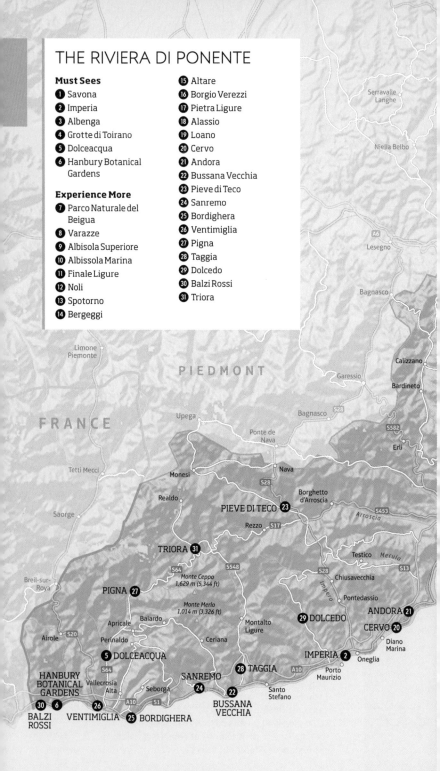

THE RIVIERA DI PONENTE

Must Sees

1 Savona
2 Imperia
3 Albenga
4 Grotte di Toirano
5 Dolceacqua
6 Hanbury Botanical Gardens

Experience More

7 Parco Naturale del Beigua
8 Varazze
9 Albisola Superiore
10 Albissola Marina
11 Finale Ligure
12 Noli
13 Spotorno
14 Bergeggi
15 Altare
16 Borgio Verezzi
17 Pietra Ligure
18 Alassio
19 Loano
20 Cervo
21 Andora
22 Bussana Vecchia
23 Pieve di Teco
24 Sanremo
25 Bordighera
26 Ventimiglia
27 Pigna
28 Taggia
29 Dolcedo
30 Balzi Rossi
31 Triora

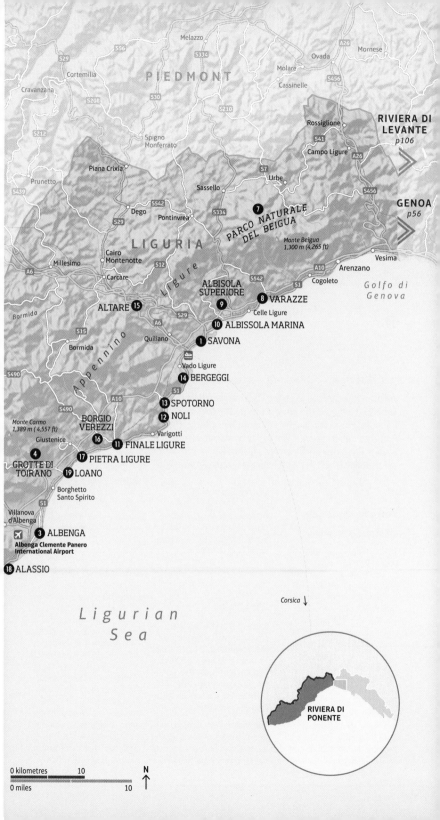

PIEDMONT

Melazzo

Cortemilia

Cravanzana

Molare

Ovada

Mornese

Cassinelle

RIVIERA DI LEVANTE
p106

Rossiglione

Spigno
Monferrato

Prunetto

Piana Crixia

Sassello

Campo Ligure

GENOA
p56

Dego

Pontinvrea

Urbe

Millesimo

Cairo
Montenotte

LIGURIA

Carcare

PARCO NATURALE
DEL BEIGUA

7

Monte Beigua
1,300 m (4,265 ft)

Vesima

Arenzano

Bormida

ALTARE **15**

Cogoleto

Golfo di
Genova

ALBISOLA
SUPERIORE

9

Celle Ligure

8 VARAZZE

Quiliano

10 ALBISSOLA MARINA

Bormida

1 SAVONA

Vado Ligure

14 BERGEGGI

Monte Cormo
1,389 m (4,557 ft)

13 SPOTORNO

Giustenice

BORGIO
VEREZZI

12 NOLI

16

Varigotti

11 FINALE LIGURE

GROTTE DI
TOIRANO **4**

17 PIETRA LIGURE

19 LOANO

Borghetto
Santo Spirito

Villanova
d'Albenga

3 ALBENGA

**Albenga Clemente Panero
International Airport**

18 ALASSIO

*Ligurian
Sea*

Corsica ↓

**RIVIERA DI
PONENTE**

0 kilometres   10

0 miles   10

N
↑

❶

SAVONA

Ⓐ C4 **FS** **ℹ️** Via Maestri d'Ascia 7r; visitsavona.com

With a name derived from the Ligurian people of the Sabates, Savona is the largest city on the Riviera di Ponente. For centuries the city was defended by the Fortezza del Priamàr, which today hosts a museum. Savona has a medieval centre, a historic port and some of the finest Art Nouveau palazzi in Liguria.

①
Torre del Brandale

Ⓐ Piazza del Brandale

The old port is an attractive part of the city, with its many sailing boats and its backdrop of medieval towers.

The 12th-century Torre del Brandale is one of the most interesting of the many old towers in Savona. It owes its name to the flagstaff on top, commonly known as the "*brandale*". Inside are traces of frescoes from the same era, while on the façade there is a ceramic relief, entitled *Apparition*, first carved in 1513 (what you see today dates from the 1960s). The tower's great bell is known to residents as "*a campanassa*". This name was coined by a local history

association whose head-quarters are in the adjacent Palazzo degli Anziani, once the seat of the *podestà*. Built in the 14th century, its façade dates from the 1600s.

---

②
Il Priamàr

Ⓐ Corso Mazzini (access from Ponte di San Giorgio) **Ⓒ Il Priamàr: 329 2104 905; Pinacoteca Civica: 019 811 520; Civico Museo Storico-Archeologico: 019 2211 770** **Ⓞ Hours vary, check website** **Ⓦ visitsavona.com**

The Priamàr fort (derived from *pietra sul mare*, or "stone above the sea") was built by Genoese rulers on the site of the first Savona settlement in the

🏔 **GREAT VIEW**
Cavallo Superiore

The lofty keep of Il Priamàr leads (via embankments and ramps) to the so-called Cavallo Superiore view point, from which there are superb views over the whole of Savona.

16th and 17th centuries. It was used as a prison in the 19th century: Giuseppe Mazzini, a key figure in the Risorgimento, was held here in 1830–31. Today, the fort houses two major museums but it is also worth a visit as a work of military architecture.

The two museums are in the fort's Palazzo Gavotti (or Palazzo della Loggia). Of these, the most important is the Pinacoteca Civica. Spread over 22 rooms on the second and third floors, it is dedicated to works by Ligurian artists from the Middle Ages to the 20th century. The third floor houses Crucifixions by Donato de' Bardi and Giovanni Mazone, and a collection of ceramics from the 12th to the 20th centuries. There is also a 15th-century polyptych (a part of which is in the Paris Louvre)

by Mazone entitled *Christ on the Cross between the Marys and St John the Baptist*. The second floor is taken up by the art collection of the late Italian president Sandro Pertini, including around 90 works by modern artists.

On the first floor of the palazzo is the Civico Museo Storico-Archeologico, which exhibits finds from the original Savonese settlement. Ceramics, amphorae and funerary objects from the Bronze and Iron ages are on display, along with medieval weaving tools, ornamental

↑ Savona majolica in the Civico Museo Storico-Archeologico, Il Priamàr

←
Boats moored at Savona, one of the most important ports in Liguria

objects and vessels. Look out for the superb Arab- and Byzantine-influenced ceramics and the Savona majolica (typically coloured blue and white). There is also a 5–6th-century burial ground.

---

③

Piazza Salineri

The heart of mercantile trading in the Middle Ages, thanks to its position by the sea, this lovely square still has traces of its former splendour, especially in the streets opening onto it: Via Orefici and Via Quarda Superiore.

Two towers rise up above the piazza: the Ghibellina, built in 1200, and the tower of the Aliberti, built in 1100. Nearby is the dilapidated 16th-century Palazzo Martinengo, which bears a curious puzzle: five proverbs have been muddled

up, and the onlooker is invited to reconstruct the sayings.

---

④

Nostra Signora di Castello

🏛 Via Manzoni ⏰10am-noon Mon-Wed

This small oratory is almost hidden from view on Corso Italia, a long street of elegant shops that, along with Via Paleocapa, was the most important road built during the expansion of Savona in the 19th century. It houses one of the finest paintings in the city – a late 15th-century polyptych of the *Madonna and Saints*, by the Lombard artist Vincenzo Foppa, completed by Ludovico Brea.

The oratory also contains what is claimed to be the world's tallest processional float, *Deposition*, built by Italian sculptor Filippo Martinengo in 1795.

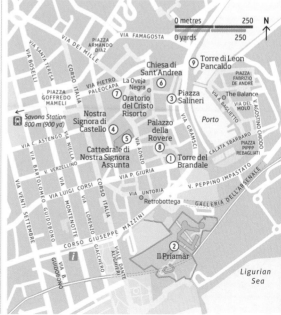

DRINK

Retrobottega

The vintage furnishings at this popular bar make for a delightfully cosy atmosphere.

⌂ Via Untoria 32r
☎ 375 782 8174

The Balance

Sample good-quality cocktails, with a special focus on tequila and mezcal, at this bar. A small selection of snacks is also available.

⌂ Via Antonio Baglietto 30r ☎ 338 540 2989

La Oveja Negra

This streetside bar offers good lagers.

⌂ Piazza dei Consoli 1/R
☎ 339 5844 609

---

⑤
Cattedrale di Nostra Signora Assunta

⌂ Piazza del Duomo

This church was built in the late 16th century to replace the old cathedral of Santa Maria del Castello, which was demolished to make space for Il Priamàr. Many of the contents of the old building were moved to the new one, including the splendid baptismal font, made from a Byzantine capital, and a late 15th-century marble *Crucifixion* – both are in the nave, behind the façade.

The church's imposing marble façade dates from the late 19th century and features, above the central door, *Assumption* by the Carrara artist Cybei (1706–84). Inside, the three aisles are divided by columns and flanked by chapels. In the presbytery is a masterpiece by Albertino Piazza, *Enthroned Madonna with Child and saints Peter and Paul*, and *Presentation of Mary at the Temple*, a marble relief

dating from the 16th century. The presbytery also has wooden choir stalls from 1515. Commissioned by the Republic of Savona and Cardinal Giuliano Della Rovere for the first cathedral, they were remodelled for the new semicircular apse.

In one of the chapels is a notable 15th-century fresco of the Madonna della Colonna. Also of interest is the pulpit of the Evangelists (1522).

To the left of the presbytery there is access to the **Museo del Tesoro della Cattedrale**, a treasury museum. The core of its collection dates from the first half of the 14th century. Other works include a polyptych, *Assumption and Saints*, by Ludovico Brea (1495), *Madonna and saints* by Tuccio d'Andria (1487) and the 16th-century *Adoration of the Magi* by the Master of Hoogstraten.

In the cloister alongside the church are 21 marble statues of saints. At the far end is Savona's own Cappella Sistina, built in 1481 for another della Rovere pope, Sixtus IV (for whom the Sistine Chapel was built), as a resting place for his parents. The interior of the chapel was transformed in the 18th century, when multicoloured stucco was introduced. The marble tomb of Sixtus IV's parents (1483) is on the left-hand side.

Museo del Tesoro della Cattedrale

◈ ⌚ 10am–12:30pm & 3:30–6pm daily (Sun pm only); book ahead except on Sat
☎ 327 0281 083

---

⑥
Chiesa di Sant'Andrea

⌂ Piazza dei Consoli

The arcaded Via Paleocapa, Savona's main shopping

←

The lofty interior of Cattedrale di Nostra Signora Assunta

street, runs inland from the Torre di Leon Pancaldo. Notice the lovely Palazzo dei Pavoni at no. 3, designed by Alessandro Martinengo.

A short distance along the street, a flight of steps leads to the 18th-century church of Sant'Andrea, built as the Jesuit church of Sant' Ignazio. Inside, there is Ratti's *Immaculate Conception* (1749) and a 16th-century *Madonna* by Defendente Ferrari. In the sacristy is an icon of *St Nicholas*, and a 19th-century *Madonna della Misericordia*, sculpted by Antonio Brilla.

↑ Torre di Leon Pancaldo, overlooking Savona's dock since the 14th century

⑦ Oratorio del Cristo Risorto

🏛 **Via Pia (off via Paleocapa)**
📞 **019 8386 306**

Further along Via Paleocapa, this oratory was reconstructed in the early 17th century as part of an existing convent of Augustinian nuns, the Santissima Annunziata. The façade is typical of many Baroque buildings in the region. The interior, where chapels face onto a single room with a barrel vault, is charming. Liberally adorning the place are 18th-century trompe l'oeil frescoes and stuccoes, which create an illusionistic background.

Traditionally, the high altar is attributed to Francesco Parodi, but he may have been responsible only for the design. In the presbytery, the statue of Cristo Risorto (Christ Arisen), to whom the oratory is dedicated, is by an unknown artist. The organ dates from 1757, and there are also some fine 15th-century choir stalls.

Maragliano's *Annunciation* (1722), the *Addolorata* (1795) by Filippo Martinengo and the *Deposition* (1866) by Antonio Brilla are three processional floats for which the oratory is famous. Many churches in Savona have floats featuring scenes from the Passion which are shown on the streets on Good Friday.

⑧ Palazzo della Rovere

🏛 **Via Pia 98**

The ancient Via Pia, which begins near the oratory, is one of the most charming streets in the old city. Hemmed in and full of shops of every description, its medieval layout has lost none of its original fascination. At the far end of Via Pia near the dock, at no. 28, is Palazzo Della Rovere, now the police headquarters. This fine palace was designed by Giuliano da Sangallo (one of the architects of St Peter's in Rome) for Cardinal Giuliano della Rovere, later Pope Julius II, in 1495. It became the property of the Spinola family and then, in 1673, was acquired by the Order of the Poor Clares. The nuns covered

Did You Know?

In 1527, the Genoese army destroyed all of Savona's city walls, but left the Torre di Leon Pancaldo standing.

up the magnificent interior decoration with plaster and renamed it Palazzo Santa Chiara. With its façade divided into three storeys with pilasters, its two-tone marble cladding, and its vast courtyard, this palazzo is a clear example of traditional Tuscan architecture.

⑨ Torre di Leon Pancaldo

🏛 **Piazza Leon Pancaldo**

This small tower at one end of the harbour is the last remnant of the 14th-century walls. It is dedicated to the Savona-born navigator who accompanied Magellan on his voyages to the Americas, and who died on the Rio della Plata in 1538.

The tower features an effigy of the *Madonna della Misericordia*, patron saint of the city, dated 1662. Beneath it is a verse by the local poet Gabriello Chiabrera, dedicated to the Madonna: *"In mare irato/In subita procella/Invoco Te/Nostra benigna stella"*, unusual because the words are the same in both Italian and Latin. In English it reads: "In this raging sea, this sudden storm, I beseech thee, oh guiding star."

The picturesque town of Oneglia, with its sun-kissed port ↑

2

IMPERIA

Ⓐ B5 🚉🚌 𝒊 Molo lungo di Oneglia; imperiaexperience.it

One of four provincial capitals in Liguria, Imperia consists of the two centres of Oneglia and Porto Maurizio, united by Mussolini in 1923. Historically rivals, the two centres are considerably less divided today, sharing one central station, though there are still two harbours and even two dialects differentiating them.

ONEGLIA

The name Oneglia probably derives from a plantation of elms (*olmi*), on which the town was originally built. Records of Oneglia date as far back as 935, when it was destroyed by the Saracens. From the 11th century it was owned by the bishops of Albenga, but they sold it to the Doria family in 1298 (Andrea Doria was born here in 1466.) The House of Savoy claimed ownership for a time, but Oneglia, along with Porto Maurizio, passed into the hands of the Genoese republic in 1746. The House of Savoy returned in 1814, and made Oneglia the provincial capital. Today, Oneglia has a thriving shopping district and busy port.

①

The Port

East of the mouth of the River Impero, the port of Oneglia (Porto di Levante) is dedicated largely to commercial trade, in particular the trade in olive oil (the town has a museum devoted to olive oil). There is also a big pasta factory on the seafront. The port, whose appearance dates mainly from the Savoy period, is the centre of activity in Oneglia. In summer (from mid-June to mid-September), look out for boats offering to take guests out to sea to watch whales and dolphins – a great experience.

②

Calata Giovan Battista Cuneo

This quay building faces the harbour, its arcades designed to shelter fishmongers and trattoria. When the boats of Oneglia's fishing fleet return from their trips out on the open sea, an auction of fresh fish is held here, usually around the middle of the afternoon. Also worth a visit are the lively local bars and restaurants.

③

Collegiata di San Giovanni Battista

🏛 Piazza San Giovanni
📞 0183 682 969 🕑 7:30am–7:30pm daily

At the heart of Oneglia's bustling shopping district, in Piazza San Giovanni, stands

Did You Know?

Oneglia has a history of trade with Marseille, and French influence can still be felt in the town's culture.

STAY

Hotel Rossini al Teatro

Enjoy a comfortable stay at the four-star Rossini al Teatro, near the harbour.

🅰 Piazza Gioacchino Rossini 14, Oneglia
🆆 hotel-rossini.it

€€€

Hotel Arc en Ciel

This family-run, ocean-facing hotel even has a private beach.

🅰 Viale Torino 39, Oneglia
🆆 hotelarcenciel.it

€€€

the Collegiata di San Giovanni Battista. This large church, the primary place of Catholic worship in Oneglia, was built in 1739–62 in late Baroque style, though the façade was finished only in 1838. The fresco decoration inside also dates from the 19th century.

Look out for the marble tabernacle (to the left of the presbytery), which dates from 1516 and is attributed to the Gagini school. Various saints are represented here and, in the lunette, *Christ Arising from the Tomb*. Also of interest are the wooden choir stalls; the *Madonna del Rosario* (in the first chapel in the left-hand aisle), attributed to the school of the 18th-century sculptor Maragliano; and *St Clare Drives out the Saracens*, a moving work painted by Gregorio De Ferrari, a native of Porto Maurizio, though he spent much of his time in Genoa.

---

④
Chiesa di San Biagio

🅰 Piazza Ulisse Calvi

This church, built in 1740, has a plain façade and a Baroque bell tower. Its spacious interior is shaped in an oval and ends in a choir. The church contains

various works such as *Gloria di San Biagio* (Glory of St Blaise) by Bocciardo and a wooden *Crucifixion* by the school of Maragliano on the altar.

---

⑤
Via Bonfante

Oneglia's main shopping street, Via Bonfante is a wonderful place for a stroll,

and for soaking up the atmosphere of the town. Beneath its 19th century arcades visitors will find art galleries and shops (including several designer boutiques), as well as inviting cafés.

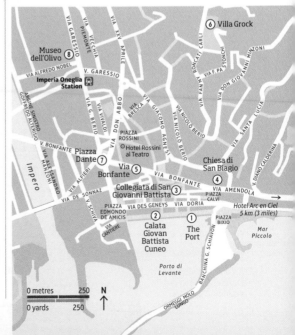

⑥
Villa Grock

🏠 18100 Via Fanny Roncati Carli 📞 0183 704 211 🕐 9:30am–12:30pm Mon, 3–6pm Thu, 5:30–10pm Fri–Sun

This Liberty-style mansion was the former home of Swiss circus artist Charles Adrian Wettach (1880–1959), better known by his stage name Grock. Juggler, musician and acrobat, he charmed audiences around the world, becoming the highest-paid circus artist of all time. Villa Grock reflects his eccentricity, with features that echo the world of the circus and include balustrades, street lamps and engravings. Today, it houses the Museo del Clown, with interactive displays, film reels starring Grock, videos revealing magic tricks and a dress-up room where children can try on colourful costumes. The villa's balconies offer stunning views out to sea. The leafy grounds are also a highlight, featuring fountains, columns, arches and a large pond.

> Housed in an old olive oil mill, the Museo dell'Olivo was opened by the Fratelli Carli, owners of just one of the many local producers of olive oil.

⑦
Piazza Dante

At the end of Via Bonfante is the central Piazza Dante, also known locally as the "Piazza della Fontana" (Square of the Fountain).

A busy crossroads, the piazza is surrounded by Neo-Medieval palazzi. Among the most interesting of these is the ex-Palazzo Comunale, at no. 4, built in the 1890s in an eclectic mix of styles.

⑧
Museo dell'Olivo

🏠 Via Garessio 13 🕐 10am–1pm & 3–6pm Tue–Sat 🌐 museodellolivo.com

Housed in an old olive oil mill, the Museo dell'Olivo was opened by the Fratelli Carli, owners of just one of the many local producers of olive oil. One part of the museum traces the history of olive cultivation, starting with the Roman period, when the oil was used more for medical and cosmetic purposes than as a food; small bottles, used to store oil as perfume or medicine, are on display. There is also a reconstruction of the hold of a Roman ship, which shows how amphorae full of olive oil were stacked ready for transportation. The main section, complete with audiovisual aids, is dedicated to explaining the production of olive oil: on display are all sorts of mills, presses, machines for filtering oil, and containers for storing and for transporting it.

A visit to the museum concludes with an optional trip to a functioning oil mill that is still being used by the local Fratelli Carli company.

The palm-shaded and elaborately landscaped grounds of Villa Grock ↑

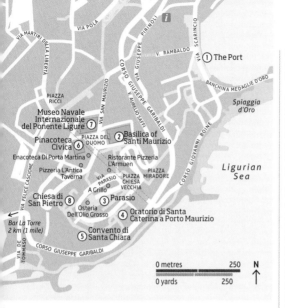

PORTO MAURIZIO

While Oneglia represents the more modern, commercial side of Imperia, Porto Maurizio is its old heart, with its long porticoes, 16th-century bastions and Baroque churches. Porto Maurizio, on the west side of the mouth of the River Impero, has retained more traces of its earlier history than Oneglia, which developed primarily in the 18th and 19th centuries. Indeed, its Centro Storico, largely a monument to the Genoese golden age, remains almost intact. Porto Maurizio fell into Genoese hands in 1797, and in 1805 was annexed, along with Genoa, to France during the Napoleonic era. Restored to the Ligurian Republic in 1814, it was united for the first time with Oneglia as part of the Kingdom of Sardinia, and in 1860 was absorbed into the Kingdom of Piemonte, under whose rule it remained until union with Oneglia in 1923.

The quarter of Parasio, the medieval part of the town, is focused around the cathedral. The two most important museums in Imperia are also found here. Porto Maurizio has two attractive coastal districts, known as Borgo Foce and Borgo Marino.

① The Port

Also known as the Porto di Ponente (to distinguish it from Oneglia's Porto di Levante), the port is protected by two piers. With its floating landing stages, the harbour is reserved for holiday yachts, and contrasts sharply with Oneglia's commercial port.

② Basilica di San Maurizio

🏠 Piazza Duomo 14
📞 0183 61901

Looking at the Basilica di San Maurizio, it should come as no surprise that this is the largest church in Liguria. It was built between 1781 and 1838 by Gaetano Cantoni in Neo-Classical style to replace the old parish church of San Maurizio, which had been demolished.

The impressive façade features eight Doric columns, culminating in a drum flanked by two solid bell towers, which form a portico. Beneath the portico are statues that once belonged to the old parish church.

The impressive interior, built on a Greek cross plan, contains a rich array of 19th-century canvases and Neo-Classical frescoes, the work of painters mostly from Liguria and nearby Piemonte. Among the highlights here is a *Predica di San Francesco Saverio*, attributed to De Ferrari. In the third chapel on the left, there is a beautiful wooden cross by the renowned school of Maragliano, while the second chapel on the right contains an intricate statue of the *Madonna della Misericordia*, which also came from the demolished San Maurizio.

DRINK

Bar La Torre
Enjoy an aperitivo as the sun sets at this bar with seafront seating.

🏠 Via Lamboglia, Porto Maurizio
📞 338 465 0074

Enoteca Di Porta Martina
This is the perfect choice for an informal bite or simply for a glass or two of local wine. Check the blackboard to see what's available.

🏠 Via Gustavo Straff-
orello 36, Porto Maurizio
🌐 enotecadi-
portamartina.it

③
Parasio

Visitors cannot truly claim to have seen Imperia unless they have explored Parasio's streets. The former palace of the Genoese governor was known in the local dialect as "Paraxu" (Ligurian for Palatium, as in Palatine Hill, in Rome). Translated into Italian, this became Parasio, the name now given to Porto Maurizio's medieval district. The palace was built on the top of the hill, in Piazza Chiesa Vecchia, now at the heart of the district and only a short walk from the Piazza del Duomo, along Via Acquarone. After a long period of neglect, Parasio has been the subject of an ambitious restoration project. In Via Acquarone, look out for the striking Palazzo Pagliari (built 1300–1400).

④
Oratorio di Santa Caterina a Porto Maurizio

🏛 Via S Maurizio 📞 5235 0107 🕐 7:30am-6:30pm daily (Sun: from 8:30am; winter: to 6pm)

In the southern part of Parasio, looking out towards the sea, this oratory (1600) is dedicated to Imperia's official patron saint. Inside

⛰ GREAT VIEW
Parasio Streets

The charming streets and paths of the Parasio area are steep, with countless viewpoints offering panoramas out over the sea and the mountains. Climb to the palace at the top for the greatest views.

is a lovely work, *Our Lady of Sorrows and Souls in Purgatory*, by Gregorio De Ferrari (1647–1726).

St Leonard (1676–1751) was born in the house that stands next to the oratory.

⑤
Convento di Santa Chiara

🏛 Via Santa Caterina 9 📞 01 83 62762 🕐 7am-9:30pm daily (Sun: to 9:15pm)

The principal reason to visit these buildings, which date from 1300 (modified in the 18th century), is to see the splendid arcade behind the convent, from which there is a fantastic view of the sea, and which is used to stage classical concerts in summer. Inside the church are two significant pieces of art: *San Domenico Soriano and Madonna*, the work of

Domenico Fiasella, and *Madonna with Child and Santa Caterina da Bologna*, by Sebastiano Conca.

⑥
Pinacoteca Civica

🏛 Piazza Duomo 11 📞 0183 61136 🕐 Sep-Jun: 4-7pm Wed, Sat & Sun; Jul & Aug: 9pm-midnight Wed, Sat & Sun

Located in Piazza del Duomo is the entrance to the Pinacoteca Civica, the municipal art gallery. On display here are collections derived from legacies and various donations, but exhibitions of local work are held here, too. Housed in the gallery are works of note by Barabino, Rayper, Frascheri and Semino, among others. The paintings form part of

←
Still blue waters glimpsed from Convento di Santa Chiara's arcade

↑ Brightly coloured buildings lining the streets of Porto Maurizio

A Grillo

A tastefully furnished restaurant nestled in the old heart of Parasio, A Grillo has an extensive wine list and specializes in Italian dishes.

🏠 Via Carceri Vecchie 19, Porto Maurizio
🌐 ristoranteagrillo.it

€€€

Osteria Dell'Olio Grosso

This cosy spot offers a wide variety of local delicacies. Start by sampling the excellent homemade ravioli.

🏠 Via Parasio 36, Porto Maurizio
📞 0183 60815

€€€

Ristorante Pizzeria L'Armuen

A popular local establishment, Ristorante Pizzeria L'Armuen offers simple dishes best enjoyed alfresco.

🏠 Via S Leonardo 14, Porto Maurizio
📞 347 941 7856

€€€

Pizzeria L'Antica Taverna

At this pizzeria, tuck into affordable pizza and delectable seafood served by friendly staff: a winning combination.

🏠 Via Giosuè Carducci 63, Porto Maurizio
📞 0183 62130

€€€

the Rebaudi collection, which also includes 19th-century Ligurian and Genoese works.

⑦ Museo Navale Internazionale del Ponente Ligure

🏠 Piazza Duomo 11
📞 0183 651 541 ⏰ 3:30-7pm Wed & Sat (9am-11am Tue, Tues: for school groups only)

Set in Piazza del Duomo is Imperia's naval museum, Museo Navale Internazionale del Ponente Ligure. This is one of the most intriguing institutions in the city, not to be missed by anyone with an interest in seafaring.

The museum is divided into various sections and includes fascinating dioramas and models of ships. The section that deals with everyday life on board a ship is very popular and is worth exploring. There are also displays of various historical documents and other mementoes relating to the seafaring tradition along the Riviera di Ponente. The museum has a specialist nautical library and archive.

⑧ Chiesa di San Pietro

🏠 Salita San Pietro
📞 0183 60356 ⏰ Jun-Aug: 9-11pm Fri-Sun; by appt only

This pretty Parasio church, the oldest religious building in Imperia, stands on the same level as a loggia overlooking the sea. Founded in 1100, it was built on the ruins of the old town walls. A medieval lookout tower forms the base of the round bell tower.

The façade, dating from 1789, is strikingly designed, with paired columns supporting three arches. A pictorial cycle on the *Life of St Peter*, attributed to Italian artists Tommaso and Maurizio Carrega (late 1700s), can be admired from inside the church.

The Roman town of Albingaunum with Albenga over the River Centa ↑

ALBENGA

C5 FS i Piazza del Popolo; www.albenga.net

In the province of Savona, Albenga is one of the Riviera di Ponente's most important cities. The Roman town of Albingaunum was founded on the site of a port built by the Ligurian Ingauni people. Today, Albenga has one of the best-preserved historic centres in Liguria and is surrounded by lush and fertile plains.

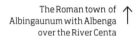

①
Palazzo
Peloso Cepolla

Piazza San Michele

Originally made up of several buildings, the Palazzo Peloso Cepolla was unified in a late-Renaissance building in the 17th century. The building is dominated by a Romanesque tower. The palazzo is home to the **Museo Navale Romano**. Its most important finds include more than 1,000 amphorae, vases and other objects found on board the wreck of a Roman ship which sank off the coast of Albenga in the 1st century BCE.

Museo Navale Romano
0182 51215 10am–12:30pm & 2:30–6pm Tue–Sun

②
Cathedral of
San Michele

Piazza San Michele 12
8am–7pm daily

Overlooking Albenga's main square, the cathedral is the old seat of both civil and religious authority. It has been remodelled several times since its construction in the Middle Ages (on the site of an Early Christian church), but remnants of the Romanesque building survive. The interior was returned to its simple 13th-century form by restoration work carried out in the 1960s. Highlights inside include a fresco of the *Crucifixion with Saints* (1500), an enormous 19th-century organ and the Carolingian crypt.

③
Palazzo Vecchio
del Comune

Via Nino Lamboglia 1

This building dates from the early 14th century and, with the Torre Comunale, forms a great medieval complex. The cathedral tower, the Torre Comunale and the tower of the Palazzo Vecchio itself are known as "Preghiera" (Prayer), "Governo" (Government) and "Giustizia" (Justice), respectively. At the top of the Palazzo Vecchio's tower is a bell known as the *campanone*, cast in 1303. Within the complex, the **Civico Museo Ingauno** has finds dating from the pre-Roman era to the Middle Ages. Objects include mosaics, tombstones and sculptures.

Civico Museo Ingauno
0182 568 5216
9:30am–1pm & 2:30–6:30pm Tue–Sun; Mon: by appt only

> At the top of the Palazzo Vecchio's tower is a bell known as the *campanone*, cast in 1303.

④
Baptistry

📍 Piazza San Michele
🕐 9:30am–1pm & 2:30–6:30 pm Tue–Sun; by appt only Mon

Albenga's most important monument is also the only remaining evidence of the Early Christian era in the whole of Liguria. It is thought to have been founded by Constantius, general to the emperor Honorius, in the 5th century. Restoration work completed in the 20th century returned the building to its original appearance. Unusually, the Baptistry takes the form of an irregular decagon outside, and a regular octagon inside. There is a niche in each of these eight sides, with columns of Corsican granite topped by Corinthian capitals supporting the arches above. The entrance to the Baptistry is through one of these niches, while others function as windows – two of the latter feature beautiful sandstone transennas. On the altar niche is *Trinity and the Apostles*, a 5th–6th century mosaic in Byzantine style; in another is a Romanesque fresco of the Baptism of Christ. At the centre is an octagonal font, with 5th-century frescoes. Tickets include access to Civico Museo Inguano.

---

⑤
Palazzo Vescovile

📍 Piazza San Michele

This palazzo, whose principal façade faces the Baptistry, is an assembly of medieval buildings, rebuilt in the 16th century. The oldest wing, to the far right, dates from around 1000, while a 12th-century tower rises from the left-hand corner. The Palazzo Vescovile is now home to the **Museo Diocesano d'Arte**

↑ Interior of the octagonal font at the Baptistry in Albenga

Sacra, where visitors can view precious church furnishings, illuminated manuscripts, Flemish tapestries, silverware and some fine works of art, including *Martyrdom of St Catherine* by Guido Reni, *Annunciation* by Domenico Fiasella and *Last Supper* by Domenico Piola, all painted in the 17th century.

Museo Diocesano d'Arte Sacra
📷 📞 0182 555 997 🕐 9:30am–12:30pm & 3:30–6:30pm Tue–Sat (winter: 9:30am–12:30pm & 3–6pm Tue–Sat)

⑥
Isola Gallinara

📍 Riserva Naturale Regionale dell'Isola Gallinara 🌐 www.parks.it

Off the coast between Albenga and Alassio is Isola Gailinara, whose name derives from the wild hens (*galline*) that used to live here. St Martin of Tours found refuge here in the 4th century and Benedictine monks founded an abbey – its ruins are still visible. The 16th-century Torre di Vedetta, built by the Republic of Genoa, stands at the top of the island. Isola Gallinara is now a nature reserve with a large population of herring gulls; it can still be admired from a boat trip.

Did You Know?

Albenga is also known as the "city of a hundred towers".

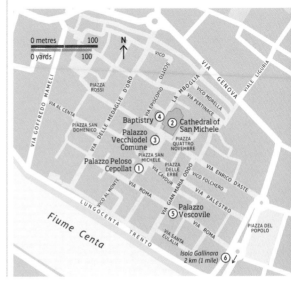

A SHORT WALK
ALBENGA

Distance 550 m (0.3 miles) **Time** 7 minutes
Nearest station Stazione di Albenga

In the old heart of Albenga, with its superb collection of medieval piazzas, palazzi and churches, the streets are set at intersecting right angles, reflecting the grid layout of the *castrum* (or military camp) of the early Roman town. With its plethora of red-brick tower-houses – some still standing proud, some much reduced, and many now restored – the historic centre of Albenga is utterly delightful. This rare example of a medieval city built on Roman foundations is undoubtedly one of the top places to visit in the whole of Liguria, and a walk through its streets is the best way to experience it.

A solid bastion called Il Torracco, once used as a prison, projects from the northwest corner of the city wall. Alongside is 17th-century **Porta Torlaro**.

START

VIA TORLARO

VIA DELLE MEDAGLIE D'ORO

PIAZZA ROSSI

VIA B RICCI

The **Lengueglia Doria Tower and House** *lie at the end of Via Ricci. The tower dates from the 13th century, while the brickwork house was built in the 15th century.*

PIAZZA SAN DOMENICO

VIA CAVOUR

VIA ROMA

Via Bernardo Ricci, *lined with intact or restored medieval houses, is Albenga's most picturesque street. In the Roman era it formed part of the main road, or decumanus maximus.*

← Charming Via delle Medaglie d'Oro, in the heart of Albenga

Olive trees outside an oil press in Albenga

Locator Map

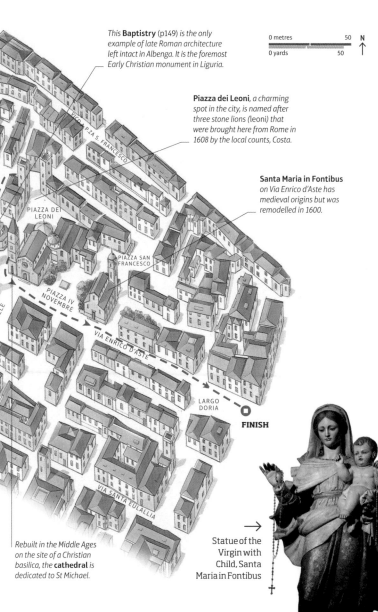

This **Baptistry** (p149) is the only example of late Roman architecture left intact in Albenga. It is the foremost Early Christian monument in Liguria.

Piazza dei Leoni, a charming spot in the city, is named after three stone lions (leoni) that were brought here from Rome in 1608 by the local counts, Costa.

Santa Maria in Fontibus on Via Enrico d'Aste has medieval origins but was remodelled in 1600.

0 metres   50

0 yards   50

N

FINISH

Rebuilt in the Middle Ages on the site of a Christian basilica, the **cathedral** is dedicated to St Michael.

Statue of the Virgin with Child, Santa Maria in Fontibus

PICTURE PERFECT
**Beyond
the Caves**

For breathtaking
views of the rock face
and landscape, linger
on the road up to the
caves. Get the perfect
shot of karst rock
giving way to the
steep valley below.

Light playing off one of ↑
the underwater pools of
Grotte di Toirano

4 ⬡ ⬡ ⬡

GROTTE DI TOIRANO

🅰 C5 🏠 Via alle Grotte 1, Toirano 🕐 Caves and Museo Etnografico Toirano: 9am–5pm daily (book ahead) 🌐 toirano.it

Situated in the karst area of the Val Varatella, between Albenga and Pietra Ligure, are the Grotte di Toirano. This cave system, which contains impressive rock formations and Aragonite flowers, is a real wonder of nature and among the most beautiful in Italy.

Discovered by researchers and speleologists from Toirano in 1950, these subterranean caves are full of broad caverns, stalactites and stalagmites of all sizes, as well as rare crystal formations. The site, which is about 1 km (half a mile) in length, can be toured in around 90 minutes, and is one of the greatest attractions of the western Riviera. Of prime importance is the beautiful Grotta della Bàsura ("Cave of the Witch" in Ligurian dialect), where traces of Palaeolithic humans have been found. There is also the Bear Cemetery, where footprints of the extinct *Ursus spelaeus* (cave bear) can be seen, and the Corridoio delle Colonne, whose fractured rocks hold evidence of ancient earthquakes. The caves are also the habitat of a small crawfish (Niphargus), while the largest ocellated lizards in Europe can also be seen near the caves.

PREHISTORIC LIGURIA

The rocky coast, with vertical cliffs facing the sea, made Liguria an attractive destination for our ancient ancestors. The rise and fall of the sea level, over the course of millennia, has caused the emergence and disappearance of hundreds of caves, which have been inhabited by humans since the prehistoric era. As well as offering shelter and food, Liguria also provided a series of staging posts between the coast and the hinterland and the Po Valley.

Grotte di Toirano's cave system ↓

Sala dei Misteri has balls of clay, which were likely hurled at the cave walls ceremonially.

Sala del Pantheon contains a stalagmite which reaches the great height of 8m (26 ft)

Grotta della Bàsura

The Grotta della Bàsura route starts in Sala Morelli.

Corridoio delle Colonne

Entrance

Further into the cave system is the area known as the Salotto ("Drawing Room").

The Bear Cemetery

Grotta di Santa Lucia Superiore

Toirano's landscape is characterized by steep-sided walls of karst rock.

5

DOLCEACQUA

A5 FS *i* Via Barberis Colomba 3; closed 1 May, 25 Dec; www.dolceacqua.it

Nestled in the Val Nervia hills, Dolceacqua is a delightful medieval village. Its quaint alleys wind concentrically around the central castle, with the stunning Ponte Vecchio bridge spanning the River Nervia. Today, the village is filled with boutique hotels, chic shops and art galleries.

Picturesque Dolceacqua spreads out on the slopes of the mountain and is reminiscent of one of Liguria's traditional *presepi* (nativity scenes) when seen from above. The River Nervia divides it into two quarters. On one side is Borgo, the older part, with winding medieval alleys and houses built in the 15th century. The newer district is called Terra, with numerous hotels, small bars and hostels.

The village is overlooked by the ruined Castello dei Doria, built to defend the town in 1100 and bought by the wealthy Doria family in 1270. It was famously painted by the artist Claude Monet, who loved this area.

Did You Know?

Monet described the Ponte Vecchio that links the two quarters as a "jewel of lightness".

The Ponte Vecchio has a single ogee arch spanning 33 m (110 ft). Built in the 15th century, the bridge links Terra and Borgo, separated by the River Nervia.

DOLCEACQUA'S FINEST WINE

The Rossese grape, sometimes known as Rossese di Dolceacqua, is an ancient red grape variety, primarily grown in Dolceacqua. The grape dates back to the Romans, and is strongly influenced by the hilly terrain in which it is grown, with a vibrant ruby red colour and an aroma of raspberry and cherry. While it remains relatively unknown on the international wine scene, it is highly prized among locals and visitors to Liguria.

↑ The village of Dolceacqua by the River Nervia

↑ The elegant Ponte Vecchio arching across the River Nervia

The 12th-century Castello dei Doria acquired the look of a noble palazzo over the years. It was damaged in 1754 but was dealt its final blow by the earthquake in 1887.

The Doria family settled in Palazzo Doria in the 18th century. An old passageway still links the palazzo to the church of Sant'Antonio, a route that was reserved for the Doria family alone.

The bell tower of Sant'Antonio Abate forms part of the village's encircling walls.

The church of Sant'Antonio Abate dates from 1400, but was altered in the Baroque era. Inside, there is a lovely polyptych painted by Ludovico Brea.

6 🔧 💻 🏛

HANBURY BOTANICAL GARDENS

🅰 A6 🏠 Corso Montecarlo 43, La Mortola 🚉 Ventimiglia 🕐 Mar-early-Jun & early-Sep-early-Oct: 9:30am-6pm daily (last adm: 5pm); mid-Jun-mid-Sep: 9:30am-7pm daily (last adm: 6pm); mid-Oct-28 Feb: 9:30am-5pm daily (last adm: 4pm) 🚫 25 Dec 🌐 giardinihanbury.com

The Hanbury Botanical Gardens were founded in 1867 by Sir Thomas Hanbury, a rich English businessman, and his brother Daniel, a botanist. In its early years, the gardens' rare plants were subjects for scientific, economic and pharmacological study. Today, the resplendent gardens are open to visitors and feature a dizzying array of tropical plants and flowers, thriving in the Ligurian climate.

Sir Thomas Hanbury was passionate about Liguria, and saw the opportunity that its warm climate provided. He realized he could acclimatize the tropical plants that he brought back from his travels, particularly those from hot, dry areas such as southern Africa and Mexico, and nurture them to co-exist with the existing local flora. By 1898, the gardens included more than 7,000 plant species. The gardens were left to decay during much of the 20th century but have now been coaxed back to their former glory by the University of Genoa.

The Dragon Fountain has a mysterious air to it. It is encircled by tropical papyruses; sitting on its rim is a sculpted dragon.

The Classical-style Temple of the Four Seasons is one of many temples that Sir Thomas had built around the gardens.

↑ The intricate Dragon Fountain at the gardens

↑ Hanbury Botanical Gardens

Looking out over the Villa towards the sea, and *(inset)* the Portuguese squill *(Scilla peruviana)* in full bloom

The Viale dei Cipressi *(Avenue of Cypresses)* is one of the most charming parts of the garden, with its lines of tall trees.

In the Terraces, plants are grouped so that they form themed gardens. The views from the Pavilion are superb.

The Villa, a 14th-century palazzo with great views, was where Mussolini and General Franco met in the 1930s.

TOP 4

PLANTS TO SPOT IN THE GARDENS

Eucalyptus
Look out for the delightful forest of Australian eucalyptus.

Roses
In the "Giardinetti" section, an array of roses and peonies grow.

Bamboo
The focal point of the Japanese Garden are the tall shoots of bamboo.

Citrus fruits
The gardens' impressive collection of citrus fruits consists of around 73 varieties.

EXPERIENCE MORE

7

Parco Naturale del Beigua

🅐D4 🚉Genoa/Savona 🔵🚌 ℹ️Ente Parco del Beigua: Piazza Beato Jacopo 1-3, Arenzano; www. parcobeigua.it

This densely forested area is the largest of the region's three national parks. Covering an area of 17,000 ha (42,000 acres), east of Varazze, it takes its name from Monte Beigua. The grassy plain at the mountain summit provides a platform for wonderful views and is a starting point for numerous walks.

The park's rocky heart is typically composed of ophiolites, also known as "green rocks" – metamorphic rocks derived from changes which occurred in the original igneous rock. Prehistoric axes and utensils found in this area are on display, at the Museo Civico di Archeologia in Pegli (p95). Prehistoric graffiti has also been found in Monte Beigua.

The flora and fauna in the park are extremely varied. In terms of the flora, there are vast numbers of beeches, and the Alpine aster (*Aster alpinus*) is also common. Drosera (*Drosera rotundifolia*), an insect-eating carnivorous plant, can be found in the wetland area known as the Riserva del Laione. There is also the scented daphne (*Daphne cneorum*), whose characteristic pink flowers have been chosen as the symbol of the park. The diverse wildlife includes foxes, badgers, weasels, wild boar and roe deer. Two endemic species of amphibian – *Salamandrina terdigitata* and *Triturus vulgaris meridionalis* – have also been seen here. From the southern slopes, visitors can see migratory birds in spring.

The headquarters of the Parco Naturale del Beigua is in Sassello, a pretty town on the park's western fringes.

Trekking through the vast Parco Naturale del Beigua, and *(inset)* a pretty swallowtail butterfly at the park

8

Varazze

🅐D4 🚉Savona 🔵🚌 ℹ️Corso Matteotti 56, www.comune. varazze.sv.it

At the eastern end of the Riviera di Ponente, Varazze is a seaside resort complete with a beach and palm-shaded promenade.

The town's name derives from the Roman name of *Varagine* ("trees"), though it was later known as *Ad Navalia* ("At the shipyards"). Both names were appropriate since much of the local wood was used for boat-building. The town was the birthplace of Jacobus de Varagine, a famous 13th-century friar and writer, and later a saint.

In the old centre, sights of interest include the church of

💬 INSIDER TIP
Hiking the Park

Alta via dei Monti Liguri, a 442-km- (275-mile-) long hiking trail split into 43 stages, crosses the Parco Naturale del Beigua. The trail goes from Ventimiglia to Bolano, and is popular with mountain bikers.

Sant'Ambrogio, dating from 1535. Remaining from an earlier 14th-century construction is an imposing brick bell tower in the Lombard style, complete with a spire. The Neo-Renaissance façade, in Finale stone, was built in 1916. The façade of an earlier, Romanesque church dedicated to Sant'Ambrogio has been incorporated, curiously, into the town walls, an impressive work dating from the 12th century.

Built in 1419, but much modified since, the church of San Domenico is famous as the home of the silver urn that has the remains of Jacobus de Varagine. There is also a 16th-century polyptych depicting *Blessed Jacopo and other saints*, by Simone da Pavia, and a 12th-century fresco, probably of the Sienese school, with a *Madonna delle Grazie*. A cannon ball, fired from a French ship in 1746, is embedded in the church façade.

From San Domenico, visitors can enjoy a lovely seafront walk along disused railway tracks; various paths en route cut inland up to Monte Beigua.

Celle Ligure, 3 km (2 miles) west of Varazze, is a small fishing village with twisting *caruggi* (narrow streets). The tradition of painting the houses in bright colours began so that sailors could identify them while still at sea.

The Deserto di Varazze, 9 km (6 miles) inland from Celle Ligure, is another lovely spot. It is a simple 17th-century hermitage associated with the barefoot Carmelite friars, and surrounded by a dense wood.

9

Albisola Superiore

🅰C4 🚉Savona 🚌🚍 🛈IAT Albisola Superiore, Piazza Libertà 19; www.albisola-turismo.it

Known to the Romans as Alba Docilia, Albisola consists of two parts – Albissola Marina, on the coast, and Albisola Superiore, a short way inland. Since the 15th century they have both enjoyed fame for their ceramics, made from the local clay, and typically decorated in blue and white.

Albisola Superiore's heritage can be seen in traces of a vast Roman villa, occupied from the 1st to 5th centuries CE. The parish church of San Nicolò was reconstructed in 1600 in the shadow of the castle, now in ruins. The Baroque wooden statues inside were carved by Maragliano and Schiaffino.

Within a large park stands Villa Gavotti, built in 1739–53 for the last doge of Genoa, Francesco Maria I della Rovere. The sumptuous interior has local ceramics and stuccoes by the Lombard School. The villa is home to the **Museo della Ceramica Manlio Trucco**, which has ceramics from the 16th century onwards. Displays include work by artists from Albisola and elsewhere in Liguria.

Museo della Ceramica Manlio Trucco

🏠Corso Ferrari 193 📞019 48 2 295 🕐8:30am-12:30pm Wed-Fri, 8:30am-12:30pm & 5:30-7:30pm Sat

---

10

Albissola Marina

🅰C4 🚉Savona 🚌🚍 🛈IAT Albissola Marina, Piazza Lam; www. comune. albissolamarina.sv.it

This coastal town, also known as Borgo Basso, has prospered historically due to its ceramics industry, but it is also a well-known seaside resort.

Of interest in the old town is the Forte di Sant'Antonio, known as the Castello and Piazza della Concordia in front of the parish church. Another unmissable sight is the 18th-century **Villa Faraggiana**, formerly Palazzo Durazzo. The gardens feature grottoes and statuary, including nymphs and sculptures of the god Bacchus and goddess Diana.

Villa Faraggiana

♿ 🏠Via Salomoni 117-119 🕐Hours vary, check website 🌐villafaraggiana.it

→
Elegant ceramic wares displayed at a shop in Albissola Marina

SHOP

Ceramiche Guarino
This pottery shop showcases vases, ceramics and furniture made by owner Francesco Guarino.

🅰C4 🏠Corso Giuseppe Mazzini, Albisola Superiore 🌐ceramicheguarino.com

---

Albisola Bottega Artigiana Mi-Art
Come for a variety of handcrafted majolica and terracotta items.

🅰C4 🏠Via Cristoforo Colombo 4, Albisola Superiore 🌐mi-art.it

Ceramiche Pierluca
Along with local designs, you'll find contemporary ceramics by international designers.

🅰C4 🏠Via Italia 25 Albissola Marina 🌐ceramichepierluca.it

EAT

U Fùndegu d'a Monica
This restaurant offers subtle variations of traditional Ligurian cuisine.
C4 Via Cavour 33, Spotorno 327 351 6544

€€€

Liliput
Going strong since 1961, Liliput celebrates Ligurian fish and seafood, and serves excellent salads.

C4 Regione Zuglieno 49, Noli 019 748 009

€€€

⓫
Finale Ligure

C5 Savona FS 🚌
Via San Pietro 14, Finalemarina; www.comunefinaleligure.it

One of the main towns on the Riviera di Ponente, Finale Ligure consists of the three separate townships of Pia, Marina and Borgo, which were united in 1927. Finalemarina, the buzzing resort overlooking pebbly beaches, is the modern part, while nearby Finalepia and Finalborgo, just inland, developed in the Middle Ages.

Finalepia, across the River Sciusa from Finalemarina, grew around the church of Santa Maria di Pia, which is the most important monument in the town. The grand 16th-century Benedictine abbey next door has some coloured terracottas by the Tuscan Della Robbia school.

The most interesting of the three villages is Finalborgo, whose old centre remains almost intact within its 15th-century walls. Elegant houses and palazzi abound, many now containing shops, small cafés and restaurants. The 17th-century church of San Biagio retains its Gothic bell tower, the symbol of Finalborgo.

The ex-convent of Santa Caterina is home to the **Civico Museo del Finale**, which exhibits archaeological finds from prehistoric times to the Middle Ages, including Roman-era objects.

Finale Ligure is a good base for cycling and mountain biking, with many trails. Take the road to Manie, which runs inland from Finalepia, to reach the Parco del Finalese. Limestone rock with reddish veining is found in abundance in the hinterland behind Finale, and forms an amphitheatre of cliffs in this area. Some 20 million years old, the cliffs are riddled with caves in which evidence of Palaeolithic life has been found. There are also traces of Roman and even pre-Roman roads in this area. Visitors can also see the remains of five Roman bridges, some of which are in excellent condition.

Civico Museo del Finale
♦ Chiostri di Santa Caterina, Finalborgo
⏰ Summer: 10am–1pm & 4–7pm Tue–Sun; winter: 9am–noon & 2:30–5pm Tue–Sun
🌐 museoarcheologico-delfinale.it

⓬
Noli

C4 Savona Piazza Milite Ignoto 6; www.nolitourism.it

This is one of the best-preserved medieval towns in the entire

←

Enjoying alfresco dining at the pretty cafés in Finale Ligure

The elegant interior of the church of San Paragorio, one of the highlights in Noli

region. Its good fortune began in 1097, when it assisted in the first Crusade, thereby setting itself up to become a maritime power. In the early 13th century, Noli allied itself with Genoa, and fought at her side against Pisa and Venice.

In the old town, the narrow alleys with suspended arches between the houses are reminiscent of the Centro Storico in Genoa. On Corso Italia, Noli's main street, look out for the 13th-century Torre Comunale and, next door, the Palazzo Comunale. The loggia that forms part of this palace recalls the arcades that once lined the Corso Italia.

The Cattedrale di San Pietro is medieval beneath its Baroque shell. Inside, the apse contains *Madonna enthroned with Child, angels and saints*, a polyptych by the school of Ludovico Brea. The key monument, however, is the church of San Paragorio, one of the finest examples of Romanesque design in Liguria. On the left are several Gothic tombs in Finale stone. Inside, the church has three Romanesque aisles with semicircular apses. Highlights include a vast wooden cross, a 12th-century bishop's cathedra, fragments of 14th-century frescoes and a marble pulpit.

Did You Know?

The town of Noli is famed for *cicciarelli*, or sand eels, which are fried as a local delicacy.

At the centre of the old town, focused around Via Mazzini and Via Garibaldi, rises the 17th-century parish church of the Assunta. Inside, the chapels feature frescoes by artists such as Andrea and Gregorio De Ferrari, Domenico Piola and Giovanni Agostino Ratti. There is more to see at the Oratorio della Santissima Annunziata, which has works by the Genoese school and a wooden sculpture by Maragliano, as well as curious maritime ex-votos.

13

Spotorno

A C4 **B** Savona **FS** 🚌
i Piazza Matteotti 6; www. comune.spotorno.it

Despite the extensive growth of tourism in this part of the region, which has transformed Spotorno into a large and popular resort, the town has not lost the appearance of a Ligurian fishing village, with buildings scattered along the pretty waterfront.

14

Bergeggi

A C4 **B** Savona **FS** 🚌
i Pro Loco, Via Aurelia 1; www.turismoinliguria.it

This small coastal resort lies in a lovely spot on the slopes of Monte Sant'Elena. Its strategic position and its defences enabled the town to fend off Saracen raids in the 10th and 11th centuries. In 1385, Bergeggi became the seat of a colony of deportees set up by the Republic of Genoa, which governed the town at that time.

The town is distinctive for its houses with roof terraces overlooking the sea.

The ruins of two ancient churches and a monastery can be seen on the nearby island of Bergeggi, an important religious centre in the Middle Ages. Now a nature reserve, the island is covered in thick vegetation with rocky promontories where an assortment of sea birds nest. There is also a variety of Ligurian flora on display.

15

Altare

A C4 **B** Savona

This town has been famous for the production of glass since at least the 11th century, before Murano glass from Venice came onto the scene. The **Museo del Vetro e dell'Arte Vetraria** houses both antique and modern examples, as well as objects from the local school of engraved glass, and books on the subject, some dating back 800 years old. The displays include some splendid crystal vases decorated in pure gold.

Also in the town is the church of the Annunziata and the late 17th-century Baroque church of Sant'Eugenio.

Museo del Vetro e dell'Arte Vetraria

🏠 Villa Rosa, Piazza Consolato 4, Altare
🕐 4-7pm Tue-Fri & Sun, 3-7pm Sat 🌐 museo delvetro.org

↑ Stalactites in the limestone caves of Grotte di Borgio Verezzi

16
Borgio Verezzi

🅐C5 🏠Savona 🚆💬
ℹ️ Viale Colombo 47; www.visitborgioverezzi.it

This town is formed by the two distinct centres of Borgio, on the coast, and Verezzi, on the slope above. The old cobbled streets of Borgio alternate with gardens and orchards, rising up to the 17th-century parish church of San Pietro. Near the cemetery is the pretty church of Santo Stefano, with a bell tower built of decorative brick.

A winding scenic road leads up to Verezzi. Of the four groups of houses that make up the village, all on different levels, the best preserved is Piazza, which still displays some Saracen influence. At the centre stands the church of Sant'Agostino. There is a view over the sea from one side of the church square.

Inside the limestone caves of the nearby **Grotte di Borgio Verezzi** are magical undergrounds lakes and stalactites so slim that they vibrate at the sound of a voice. Fossils of saber-tooth tigers, cave bears and elephants have been discovered here.

Grotte di Borgio Verezzi
🎨🕐 🏠Via Battorezza 📞019 610150 🕐Tours at 9:30am, 10:30am, 11:30am, 3pm, 4pm & 5pm Mon–Fri (Sat & Sun: also 2pm) 🚫25 Dec, 1 Jan

17
Pietra Ligure

🅐C5 🏠Savona 🚆💬
ℹ️ Piazza Martin Liberté 29; www.visitpietraligure.it

The name of this delightful beach resort translates as "Ligurian stone" and derives from the rocky outcrop to the northeast of the old town, where a fortified site stood in the Byzantine era. The town grew up around the base of the Castello, a Genoese stronghold that underwent alterations in the 16th century. The Borgo Vecchio was planned on a regular layout with five

> **The old cobbled streets of Borgio alternate with gardens and orchards, rising up to the 17th-century parish church of San Pietro.**

streets running parallel to the coastline. Strolling along these streets today, visitors will notice how both medieval houses and 16–17th-century palazzi rub shoulders, an unusual architectural combination that resulted from a programme of partial reconstruction in the 16th century.

The 10th-century Oratorio dei Bianchi stands in Piazza Vecchia (also known as Piazza del Mercato). In the bell tower is the "holy bronze" – according to local legend, the bell rang in 1525 to announce the end of the plague. In Piazza XX Settembre, not far from the sea, stands the 18th-century church of San Nicolò di Bari, its façade flanked by two bell towers.

18
Alassio

🅐B5 🏠Savona 🚆💬
ℹ️ Via Mazzini 68; www.visitalassio.eu

A fine sand beach, which extends for some 4 km (2 miles) and slopes almost imperceptibly down to the sea, makes Alassio the undisputed queen of the Riviera delle Palme. In the 19th century, it became a favourite holiday destination among the English, who came here and built splendid villas with gardens. Many of these, including some Art Nouveau gems, have since been turned into hotels.

Local legend has it that the town's name derives from Adelasia, daughter of Holy Roman Emperor Otto I of Saxony, who came here in the 10th century. Originally a fishing village, in the Middle Ages it became the property of Albenga and, later, of Genoa. The Roman road, Via Aurelia, still passes through it. The typically Ligurian character of

→

Colourful ceramic tiles with autographs at the Muretto in Alassio

Alassio can be seen in the long *caruggio* (narrow street) that runs parallel with the sea, hemmed in by 16th–17th-century houses and modern shops. This street is Via XX Settembre, known as the "Budello", and is the heart of the town's commercial life. From here, narrow streets known locally as *esci* fan out, leading to the seafront.

At the corner of Via Dante and Via Cavour, Caffè Roma has been a popular meeting place since the 1930s. In the 1950s, the café's owner had the idea of making ceramic tiles out of the autographs of its famous visitors to hang on the wall of the garden opposite. The Muretto now bears the signatures of many famous personalities, including Ernest Hemingway, Jean Cocteau and Dario Fo.

Alassio's most significant monument is the parish church of Sant'Ambrogio. Founded in the 1400s, it has a 19th-century façade, an early 16th-century bell tower and a Baroque interior.

At the southern end of the bay of Alassio lies Laigueglia, a seaside resort with a well-preserved and picturesque old centre. Of Roman origin, it became an important centre for coral fishing in the 16th century. A round tower, known as the Torrione circolare, the only bastion remaining of three which once protected Laigueglia from pirates, is the oldest building in the village.

The church of San Matteo has two bell towers with bright, majolica-covered cupolas, a delightful example of Ligurian Baroque.

On the ridge between Laigueglia and Andora is Colla Micheri, a hamlet whose houses were restored and made into a home by Thor Heyerdahl, the Norwegian navigator and ethnologist famous for his epic journey by raft from Peru to Polynesia in 1958. He died here in 2002.

---

⑲ Loano

🅰C5 🚉Savona 🚃💺
🛈Corso Roma 9;
www.comuneloano.it

Ever since Roman times, Loano has been a desirable place to live. Among others, the town has belonged to the bishops of Albenga, the Doria family and the Republic of Genoa. It was also the site of Napoleon's first victory in Italy. These days, Loano is an extremely pleasant town with an extensive beach.

The most interesting building is the 16th-century Palazzo Comunale, built for

the Doria family. Its austere appearance is softened by balconies and loggias, while a gallery links it to a watch tower that features a beautiful Roman mosaic pavement.

In 1603, the Doria family founded the Convento di Monte Carmelo in a lovely spot in the hills above Loano. The complex includes a church housing numerous Doria family tombs and the Casotto, a favourite Doria residence.

20

Cervo

B5 Imperia www.comune.cervo.im.it

This village, perched on a hill between Capo Cervo and the mouth of the River Cervo, signals the beginning of the province of Imperia. Once the property of the Del Carretto and then the Doria families, from the 14th century Cervo came under Genoese domination and followed that city's fortunes.

Nowadays, Cervo is an extremely pretty resort, with houses painted in white and pale shades of yellow, and overlooking a shingle beach. Dominating the village is a 12th-century castello, which belonged to the Marchesi di Clavesana and was a control point along the Via Aurelia in the Middle Ages. The site is now occupied by the **Museo Etnografico del Ponente Ligure**, which features reconstructions of life at sea and on land, together with original rooms from a local house.

Facing the sea is the parish church of San Giovanni Battista, a fine example of Ligurian Baroque. With its distinctive concave, stucco-embellished façade that features a stag (*cervo* in Italian), it was begun in 1686. The bell tower and the interior both date from the 18th century. The latter has a *St John the Baptist*, a 17th-century work in multicoloured wood by Poggio, and an 18th-century *Crucifixion* attributed to Maragliano.

Also in the town there are several interesting 17th- and 18th-century palazzi. These include Palazzo Morchio, now the town hall, and Palazzo Viale, which has 18th-century porticoes.

Museo Etnografico del Ponente Ligure

Piazza Santa Caterina 2 0183 408197 10am-1pm & 4-10pm daily (winter: 9:30am-12:30pm & 4-6pm Tue-Sat; Sun: am only

21

Andora

B5 Savona FS 🚌 Largo Milano 2; www.comune.andora.sv.it

Andora is the last coastal town at the western end of the Riviera delle Palme and is thought to have been founded by the Phocaeans from Asia Minor. Later the Romans built a bridge over the River Merula. The ten-arched Ponte Romano visible today dates, in fact, from the Middle Ages. The old Roman road leads up to the ruins of Andora Castello, which is in a lovely spot at the top of the hill. Through the castle gate is the small church of Santi Giacomo e Filippo, which was once part of the castle's extensive defences.

↑ Exterior of an antique shop, with picture frames and potted plants, in Bussana Vecchia

㉒
Bussana Vecchia

🅰B5 🅰Imperia, off Sanremo-Arma di Taggia rd

Bussana Vecchia is an atmospheric ghost town. In February 1887, an earthquake shook the village, reducing its Baroque church and surrounding houses to ruins. The town was rebuilt closer to the sea and since then the original village has been taken over by artists, who have restored some interiors, providing venues for concerts and exhibitions.

㉓
Pieve di Teco

🅰B5 🅰Imperia 🚌 🛈Piazza Brunengo 1; 0183 364 53

Heading inland, almost as far as the border with Piemonte, visitors reach the busy market town of Pieve di Teco. Founded in 1293, the town belonged, like many others in the area, to the Marchesi di Clavesana and subsequently (from the late 14th century) to Genoa.

The town is known for its handmade walking boots, as well as its small but excellent antiques market held on the

←

The village of Cervo at dusk, when its pastel-coloured houses almost seem to glow

last Sunday of the month. Two squares mark either end of the arcaded Corso Ponzoni – the heart of the town. On each side, craft workshops alternate with the palazzi of well-to-do families. The oldest part of Pieve di Teco is focused around the 15th-century church of Santa Maria della Ripa.

Also of interest is the late 18th-century collegiate church of San Giovanni Battista, which has several paintings, including *St Francis de Paul* attributed to Luca Cambiaso and *Last Supper* by Domenico Piola.

The 15th-century Convento degli Agostiniani has the largest cloister in the whole region.

㉔
Sanremo

🅰A6 🅰Imperia 🚆🚌 🛈IAT Sanremo, Palafiori, Corso Garibaldi; www.comune. sanremo.im.it

Defined by its thriving flower industry and its Festival of Italian Song, Sanremo is also one of the Italian Riviera's best-known resorts.

The city is divided into three distinct areas: Corso Matteotti and the surrounding area (the heart of the shopping district), La Pigna (the old town), and the west end of the seafront, which was the heart of the resort during its heyday. Tourism, mainly English, boomed in Sanremo

from the mid-1800s to the early 1900s, a period of great expansion when all manner of grand hotels and villas were built, including various Art Nouveau palazzi. There is no better belle époque monument than the splendid Casinò Municipale.

Another unmistakable Sanremo landmark, with its onion domes, is the Russian Orthodox Church. The Russians were almost as passionate about Sanremo as the English were, and the seafront Corso Imperatrice was named in honour of Maria Alexandrovna, wife of Tsar Alexander II and a frequent visitor to San Remo. This seafront boulevard is a favourite place to stroll.

At the end of Corso Trento e Trieste, beyond the Giardini Ormond, stands Villa Nobel, where Alfred Nobel, the famous Swedish scientist lived, and where he died in 1896.

The other part of Sanremo that no one should miss is its medieval *"città vecchia"*, fortified in the 11th century in order to keep out the Saracens. The area is known as La Pigna, or pine cone, because of its layout: the maze of alleys, steps, arches and covered walkways are spread out in concentric circles from the top of the hill. The main monuments, including the cathedral and the Oratorio dell'Immacolata Concezione are found in the central Piazza San Siro. Finally, for a fascinating insight into the local flower trade, visit Sanremo's famous wholesale flower market, which lies just east of the city centre in the Armea valley.

🔍 HIDDEN GEM
Edward Lear's Grave

Not far from the border of Sanremo, in the pretty Foce Cemetery, English poet Edward Lear is buried. His unassuming headstone proclaims he was "a landscape painter in many lands".

25 Bordighera

A6 **Imperia** FS
**Via Vittorio Emanuele II
172; www.visitbordighera.it**

The famous painting by Monet, *A View of Bordighera*, is evidence of the historic fame of this sunny and lively resort. As was the case elsewhere on the Riviera, Bordighera was particularly popular with the British. Here, too, visitors will find Art Nouveau palazzi (many converted into hotels or apartments), and a popular seafront boulevard – the Lungomare Argentina, with Capo Sant'-Ampelio at the far end. The beach is good and often busy, and dotted with palm trees.

The **Museo Clarence Bicknell** was founded by Clarence Bicknell, who was one of Bordighera's many British visitors, a vicar, botanist and an archaeologist. Bicknell's library-cum-museum houses Roman funerary objects and, more interestingly, casts of rock drawings and a vast photographic archive of ancient graffiti from the nearby Vallée des Merveilles in France. By the sea, on Capo Sant'Ampelio, is the Romanesque church of

Sant'Ampelio, with an 11th-century crypt.

In the historical centre, look out for the 17th-century church of Santa Maria Maddalena attributed to the workshop of Domenico Parodi.

For a quiet interlude, visit the **Giardino Esotico Pallanca**, which has more than 3,000 species of cacti and succulents.

Museo Clarence Bicknell
⏱ Via Romana 39
Hours vary, check website
museobicknell.com

Giardino Esotico Pallanca
⏱ Via Madonna della Ruota 1 ⏱9am-5pm Tue-Sun pallanca.it

---

26 Ventimiglia

A6 **Imperia** FS
Lungo Roja G Rossi-Angolo Via Roma; www.comune. ventimiglia.im.it

Ventimiglia is the last major town on the Riviera di Ponente before the French border. A frontier town par excellence, Ventimiglia straddles the Roia and the Nervia valleys, among the most beautiful in the Ligurian Alps.

The River Roia divides Ventimiglia into two: the medieval part on a hill to the west, and the modern town on the coastal plain to the east. Traces of the era of Roman domination, which followed rule by the Liguri Intemelii people, can be seen at **Albintimilium**, on the eastern periphery of the new town. The ruins consist of a stretch of the *decumanus maximus* (or main street), a few houses and the great baths. More important than any of these, however, is the small Theatre, the most significant

Roman monument in Liguria. Dating from the early 3rd century BCE, the theatre could seat more than 5,000 spectators. Ten levels of steps in the lower section, made from Turbia stone, are still well preserved, while the western entrance gate is practically intact. Various finds discovered at the site are on display in the nearby **Museo Archeologico Gerolamo Rossi**, in the Forte dell'Annunziata in town.

Via Garibaldi is the main street through the cobbled *centro storico*. Among the most important buildings are the Palazzo Pubblico, the Loggia del Magistrato dell'Abbondanza and the Neo-Classical former Teatro Civico. The latter houses the Civica Biblioteca Aprosiana, the oldest public library founded in 1648 in Liguria with a fine collection of rare books and manuscripts.

At the heart of Via Garibaldi is the Cattedrale dell'Assunta. This was built in place of an 8th-century Carolingian church in the 11th and 12th centuries, and has been modified at intervals since then. The bell tower, constructed on a 12th-century base, was rebuilt in the Baroque era and remodelled once again in the 19th century.

Continuing along Via Garibaldi, past another couple of churches, visitors eventually

← Cacti in the tropical Giardino Esotico Pallanca in Bordighera

↑ A picturesque view of the old town of Ventimiglia

important is the church of San Michele, founded in 1450. A splendid white marble rose window, perhaps the work of Giovanni Gagini from the early 1500s, adorns the façade. Inside the church, the *Polyptych of St Michael* is a monumental work by the Piedmontese artist Canavesio, in which the influence of painter Ludovico Brea and his artist brothers is evident. Also by Canavesio are the frescoes portraying *The Passion of Christ*, housed in the small church of San Bernardo, within the cemetery.

Other places of interest are the atmospheric ruins of the church of San Tommaso, and Piazza Castello, which offers superb views over the nearby village of Castel Vittorio.

INSIDER TIP
Train to Menton

If you fancy dipping your toes into France, it's just a 20-minute train ride from Ventimiglia to Menton, a coastal city on the French Riviera known for its seaside promenades and Menton Lemon Festival, with citrus sculptures.

reach Porta Nizza. From here, following Via della Torre and Via Appio, you reach Piazza Colletta and the lovely Romanesque church of San Michele. The main body of the church, of which only the central nave survives, dates from the 11th century. From Porta Nizza, visitors can also climb up west of the old city to the ruins of three medieval forts, a reminder of the battles that were once fought over Ventimiglia. One of these, the Castel d'Appio, built by the Genoese in the 13th century, occupies the site not only of a Roman military camp (*castrum*) but also of an early Ligurian defence post. There are marvellous views of the Riviera from here.

The modern, eastern part of Ventimiglia, complete with seaside promenades, is a shopping mecca and is very popular with the French. The streets are busy at weekends when people from the surrounding area visit for the market.

Albintimilium
🏛 Corso Genova 134 📞 0184 252 320 🕐 9:30am–2:30pm Tue–Sat & every 1st & 3rd Sun of month

Museo Archeologico Gerolamo Rossi
🖼🕐 🏛 Via Verdi 41 🕐 9am–12:30pm & 3–5pm Mon, Tue & Thu, 9am–12:30pm & 9–11pm Fri–Sun 🌐 marventimiglia.it

---

27
Pigna
🅰 A5 🏛 Imperia 🚉 Ventimiglia 🚌 ℹ Comune, Piazza Umberto I; 0184 1928 312

Situated in the foothills of the Maritime Alps in the Alta Val Nervia, some 40 km (25 miles) north of Sanremo, Pigna is a fascinating place – the town's layout is reminiscent of the eponymous district in Sanremo (*p165*). Strolling around the narrow streets, known as *chibi*, it is easy to understand how the medieval town was built, with the houses grouped on concentric streets. Among a number of fine churches, the most

EAT

Balzi Rossi
Chef Enrico celebrates Liguria with elevated takes on local recipes.

🅰 A6 🏛 Via Balzi Rossi 2, Ventimiglia 🌐 ristorantebalzirossi.it

€€€

Magiargè Osteria Contemporanea
Try the "surprise menu" for the chef's specials at this restaurant with a superb setting.

🅰 A6 🏛 Via Dritta 2, Bordighera 📞 0184 262 946

€€€

Ristorante La Musa
Traditional Italian dishes are served with expertise at this popular spot.

🅰 A6 🏛 Via Sir Thomas Hanbury 7/b, Ventimiglia 📞 0184 356 882

€€€

The impressive interior of Convento di San Domenico in Taggia, and *(inset)* its stately exterior ↑

㉘ Taggia

🅐 B5 🄰 Imperia 🔲🔳
🄸 Via Boselli, Arma di Taggia; www.taggia.it

Lying close to the mouth of the Valle Argentina is Taggia, whose 16th-century walls conceal a fascinating medieval village. One of the most impressive sights is the medieval bridge across the Argentina, with 16 arches of which two are Romanesque.

Via Soleri, the heart of the old centre, is flanked by large porticoes with black stone arches and many fine old buildings. The Baroque parish church of Santi Giacomo e Filippo is lovely and worth visiting, but Taggia's most important monument is the **Convento di San Domenico**. Built between 1460 and 1490, it is considered to have the best collection of works by the Liguria-Nice school of the 15th and 16th centuries. Its masterpieces include five works by the French artist Ludovico Brea.

Convento di San Domenico
⬦ 🄰 Piazza Beato Cristoforo
📞 018 447 6254 🄾 9am-noon & 3–6pm Mon–Sat

㉙ Dolcedo

🅐 B5 🄰 Imperia 🔳 Imperia
🔲 🄸 Piazza Doria 33; 0183 280 004

Situated in the hinterland behind Porto Maurizio is Dolcedo, a mountain village with stone-paved mule tracks and watermills along the banks of the river, evidence of an olive oil tradition dating back to the 1100s. The local olive groves are among the most famous in the region.

There are no fewer than five bridges across the river. The oldest, known as Ponte Grande, was built in 1292 by the Knights of St John.

The parish church of San Tommaso overlooks a small piazza, paved in the Ligurian style in black and white pebbles. This Baroque jewel was built in 1738.

LUDOVICO BREA

Of the many foreign artists working in Liguria between the mid-15th and the mid-16th centuries, Ludovico Brea (c.1450–c.1523) is the best documented. Born in Nice, Brea was probably influenced by the artistic trends emanating from Avignon as well as by works from different schools of European painting. Of northern European styles, he was particularly interested in Flemish art, but was also keenly interested in the miniatures found in medieval manuscripts. Brea was extremely adept at understanding the taste of his Ligurian patrons, a skill that enabled him to work in Italy for many years. After producing some early work in Nice, Brea transferred to Liguria. Traces of his life in general are scant, and generalizations about his artistic influences are usually made by studying his later work.

> **Atmospheric Balzi Rossi has yielded fascinating evidence of human settlement in this part of Liguria, going back as far as the Palaeolithic age.**

30

Balzi Rossi

🅰️ A6 🏠 Grimaldi di Ventimiglia (Imperia)

This prehistoric site, one of the most famous in the western Mediterranean, lies about 10 km (6 miles) west of Ventimiglia, below the village of Grimaldi and just a stone's throw from the Italy–France border. It consists of nine caves, which have been explored at various times since the 19th century. The name of Balzi Rossi (meaning "red rocks") derives from the reddish colour of the precipitous limestone cliffs.

This atmospheric place has yielded fascinating evidence of human settlement in this part of Liguria, going back as far as the Palaeolithic age. The area was probably chosen because of the favourable natural conditions, including the warm climate and the proximity of the sea. There is a walkway connecting several of the caves, some of which are open to the public.

Numerous stone and bone instruments, fossil remains of animals, and various ornamental objects have been discovered in the caves, in particular in the Grotta del Principe, slightly removed from the other caves and also the largest.

Of greatest interest are the many tombs, which provide a few tangible snippets of information about the people who lived here some 240,000 years ago. The most famous of these tombs, known as the Triple Tomb, was discovered in Barma Grande cave in 1892. Today, it is on display in the **Museo Preistorico dei Balzi Rossi**, founded by the Englishman Sir Thomas Hanbury in 1898. To the side

of the tomb are two male individuals, a boy and a man more than 2 m (6 ft) tall on the right. At the centre is a girl of around 16 years old. Funerary objects are shown, such as sea shells, pendants of worked bone, deer teeth and necklaces fashioned out of fish vertebrae, items that traditionally accompanied the deceased.

The museum also has on display a reproduction of the only figure engraved in a naturalistic style to be discovered at Balzi Rossi. Found in the Grotta del Caviglione, it is the profile of a shortish, stocky horse, 40 cm (16 in) long and 20 cm (8 in) high. It is known as the Przewalskii Horse; a few rare examples of the breed survive in Mongolia.

Grotte e Museo Preistorico dei Balzi Rossi

🔗🔗 🏠 Ponte San Ludovico, Via Balzi Rossi 9 📞 0184 381 13 🕐 Museum: 8:30am-7pm daily (Mon: to 1pm); Grotte: 11am-noon & 3-4pm daily

---

31

Triora

🅰️ A5 🏠 Imperia 🚉 Sanremo 🚌 ℹ️ Pro Loco, Corso Italia 7; www. comune.triora.im.it

The old medieval village of Triora, an outpost of the Republic of Genoa, lies near the head of the Valle Argentina. With the Ligurian Alps rising up behind, this is a truly enchanting place. Also known as the "paese delle streghe" (village of witches), Triora is famous above all for the witchcraft trials, held here between 1587 and 1589. The unique and popular **Museo Etnografico e della Stregoneria** is devoted to

the story of these remarkable but troubling trials.

The centre of Triora still preserves much evidence of the village's medieval origins, with little alleys, narrow streets and houses huddled together around small squares. Of seven original gates, the only survivor is Porta Soprana, with a rounded arch. Nearby is the Fontana Soprana, the oldest fountain in the town.

An unmissable sight is the collegiate church of the Assunta. It was originally Romanesque-Gothic and still retains the old bell tower and main door, though the façade is Neo-Classical. Inside there are several notable works of art, including several by Luca Cambiaso. However, chief among them is an exquisite painting on a gold background of the *Baptism of Christ* by the Sienese artist Taddeo di Bartolo. It is the oldest known painting of its type in the Riviera di Ponente.

Museo Etnografico e della Stregoneria

🔗 🏠 Corso Italia 1 🕐 3-6:30pm Mon-Fri, 10:30am-noon & 3-6pm Sat & Sun 🌐 museotriora.it

↑ Displays at the Museo Etnografico e della Stregoneria

A CYCLING TOUR
THE PISTA CICLABILE DELLA LIGURIA

Length 24 km (15 miles) **Starting points** Ospedaletti in the west or Diano Marina in the east **Stopping-off points** Each of the six towns along the route have a plethora of places to stop for refreshments

Snaking between the Mediterranean ocean and the vast mountains of western Liguria, the Pista Ciclabile is one of Europe's most popular coastal bike trails. The flat and well-maintained route follows an old railway line, running parallel to the ancient Roman Via Aurelia. As you cycle, you'll pass through six of the Riviera di Ponente's most beautiful towns and villages, cruising past affluent marinas, historic forts and numerous parks. The Riviera di Ponente's most beautiful beaches, including those around San Lorenzo al Mare and Sanremo, are also easy to reach from the route, meaning you'll have numerous reasons to stop for a well-deserved break.

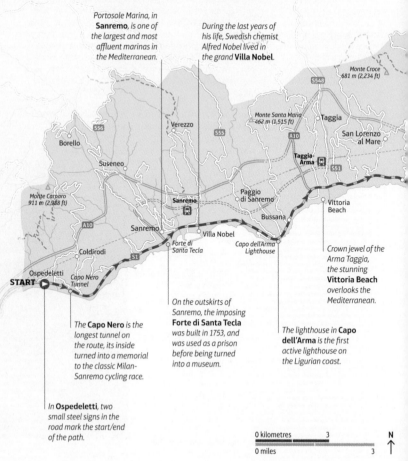

Portosole Marina, in **Sanremo**, is one of the largest and most affluent marinas in the Mediterranean.

During the last years of his life, Swedish chemist Alfred Nobel lived in the grand **Villa Nobel**.

Crown jewel of the Arma Taggia, the stunning **Vittoria Beach** overlooks the Mediterranean.

The lighthouse in **Capo dell'Arma** is the first active lighthouse on the Ligurian coast.

On the outskirts of Sanremo, the imposing **Forte di Santa Tecla** was built in 1753, and was used as a prison before being turned into a museum.

The **Capo Nero** is the longest tunnel on the route, its inside turned into a memorial to the classic Milan-Sanremo cycling race.

In **Ospedeletti**, two small steel signs in the road mark the start/end of the path.

0 kilometres 3
0 miles 3

N ↑

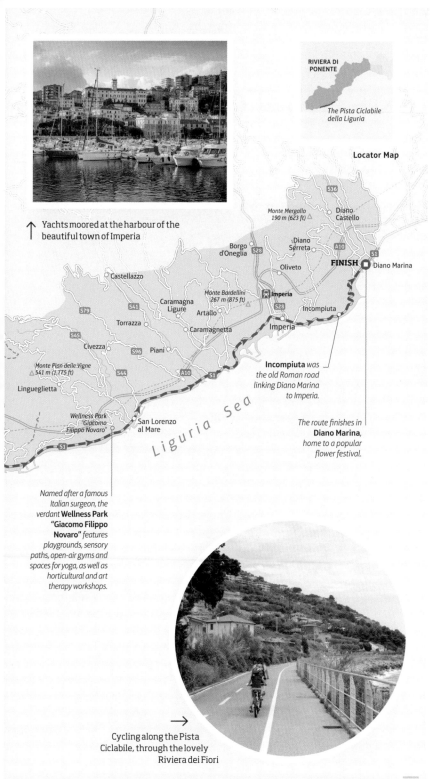

Yachts moored at the harbour of the beautiful town of Imperia

RIVIERA DI
PONENTE

The Pista Ciclabile della Liguria

Locator Map

Monte Mergallo 190 m (623 ft) △

Diano Castello

Diano Serreta

FINISH Diano Marina

Borgo d'Oneglia

Oliveto

Castellazzo

Monte Bardellini 267 m (875 ft) △

Incompiuta

Caramagna Ligure

Artallo

Imperia

Torrazza

Caramagnetta

Imperia

Incompiuta *was the old Roman road linking Diano Marina to Imperia.*

Civezza

Piani

Monte Pian delle Vigne △ *541 m (1,775 ft)*

The route finishes in **Diano Marina,** *home to a popular flower festival.*

Linguiglietta

Liguria Sea

Wellness Park "Giacomo Filippo Novaro"

San Lorenzo al Mare

Named after a famous Italian surgeon, the verdant **Wellness Park "Giacomo Filippo Novaro"** *features playgrounds, sensory paths, open-air gyms and spaces for yoga, as well as horticultural and art therapy workshops.*

→
Cycling along the Pista Ciclabile, through the lovely Riviera dei Fiori

NEED TO KNOW

Fishing boats moored near Vernazza

BEFORE
YOU GO

Things change, so plan ahead to make the most of your trip. Be prepared for all eventualities by considering the following points before you travel.

AT A GLANCE

CURRENCY
Euro (EUR)

AVERAGE DAILY SPEND

ON A BUDGET	MODERATE SPENDER	SPLASH OUT
€50	€100	€300+

BOTTLED WATER	COFFEE	BEER	DINNER FOR TWO
€1.30	€1.00	€5.00	€60

ESSENTIAL PHRASES

Hello	Buon giorno
Goodbye	Arrivederci
Please	Per favore
Thank you	Grazie
Do you speak English?	Parla inglese?
I don't understand	Non capisco

ELECTRICITY SUPPLY
Power sockets are type F and L, fitting two- and three- pronged plugs. Standard voltage is 220-230v.

Passports and Visas

For entry requirements, consult your Italian embassy or check the **Polizia di Stato** website. Citizens of the UK, US, Canada, Australia and New Zealand do not need visas for stays of up to three months but, in future, must apply in advance for the **ETIAS** (European Travel Information and Authorization System); roll-out has been continually postponed so check website. Visitors from other countries may also require an ETIAS.
ETIAS
🔳 etiasvisa.com
Polizia di Stato
🔳 poliziadistato.it

Government Advice

Now more than ever, it is important to consult both your and the Italian government's advice before travelling. The **UK Foreign, Common-wealth and Development Office** (FCDO), the **US State Department**, the **Australian Department of Foreign Affairs and Trade**, and the **Italian Ministero della Salute** offer information on security, health and local regulations.
Australian Department of Foreign Affairs and Trade
🔳 smartraveller.gov.au
Ministero della Salute
🔳 salute.gov.it
UK Foreign, Commonwealth and Development Office (FCDO)
🔳 gov.uk/foreign-travel-advice
US State Department
🔳 travel.state.gov

Customs Information

You can find information on laws relating to goods and currency on the **Your Europe** website.
Your Europe
🔳 europa.eu

Insurance

We recommend that you take out a comprehensive insurance policy covering theft,

loss of belongings, medical care, cancellation and delays, and read the small print carefully. EU, UK and Australian citizens are eligible for free emergency medical care in Italy provided they have a valid EHIC (European Health Insurance Card), or **GHIC** (UK Global Health Insurance Card).

GHIC
w ghic.org.uk

Vaccinations

No inoculations are required to visit Italy.

Booking Accommodation

Liguria offers a wide range of accommodation, from five-star hotels to B&Bs and campsites. Book well ahead if you're travelling in summer, especially at weekends, when the coast fills up with weekenders from Milan and Turin.

Money

Most establishments accept major credit, debit and pre-paid currency cards. Contactless payments are common in the Riviera, but it's always a good idea to carry cash for smaller items and ticket machines at stations. Wait staff should be tipped €1–2 and hotel porters and housekeeping will expect €1 per bag or day.

Travellers with Specific Requirements

The hilly terrain and steep cobbled streets mean that Liguria can pose a challenge for travellers with mobility issues, but there are local services at hand to help. Today, 10 *comuni* in Liguria belong to the **Bandiera Lilla** project which aims to make beaches accessible, and the tourist board works with the **Lamia** disability charity to produce an annual list of the region's accessible beach clubs.

The rail network is excellent, and assistance can be booked on and off trains. The towns and villages are more of an issue themselves, as they tend to be hilly – Genoa's Centro Storico is steep and the Cinque Terre villages are built on hills (Riomaggiore has a lift, but it doesn't always work, particularly out of season). Ask your accommodation for advice about getting

around. In general, the Riviera di Ponente is more accessible.

Bandiera Lilla
w bandieralilla.it
Lamia
w lamialiguria.it

Language

Italian is the official language. The level of English and other foreign languages spoken is generally good in the tourist hotspots, but in the Riviera's rural areas less so, and locals appreciate visitors' efforts to speak Italian, even if its only a few words.

Opening Hours

Situations can change quickly and unexpectedly. Always check before visiting attractions and hospitality venues for up-to-date opening hours and booking requirements.

Lunchtime Some smaller shops and bars close during or shortly after lunchtime.
Sundays Most shops outside of the main cities are closed, and public transport services are generally reduced.
Mondays Many museums and tourist attractions and some restaurants are closed for the day, particularly in quieter towns.
Public holidays Schools, post offices and banks are closed.

PUBLIC HOLIDAYS

1 Jan	New Year's Day
6 Jan	Epiphany
4 Apr	Easter Sunday
5 Apr	Easter Monday
25 Apr	Liberation Day
1 May	Labour Day
2 Jun	Republic Day
15 Aug	Ferragosto
1 Nov	All Saints Day
25 Dec	Christmas Day
26 Dec	St Stephen's Day

GETTING AROUND

Whether exploring the region by foot, by bike or public transport, here is everything you need to know to navigate like a pro.

AT A GLANCE

PUBLIC TRANSPORT COSTS

GENOA LIFTS AND FUNICULARS
€0.90
Single journey

CINQUE TERRE TRAIN
€5.00
Single journey

SAVONA TO VENTIMIGLIA
€12.10
Single journey
by train

SPEED LIMIT

MOTORWAY
130 km/h (80m/h)

DUAL CARRIAGEWAYS
110 km/h (70m/h)

NATIONAL ROADS
90 km/h (50m/h)

URBAN AREAS
50 km/h (30m/h)

Arriving by Air

Genova City Airport is Liguria's only international airport. Pisa Airport is about an hour (by train or car) south of La Spezia, while just across the border, Nice Côte d'Azur is just 45 minutes from Ventimiglia. Milan Linate is under two hours from Genoa, and Turin another 30 minutes (both are easily reached by train or coach). For more information on getting into town from Genoa airport, see the table opposite.

Train Travel

International Train Travel
Regular high-speed international trains connect Italy to the main towns and cities in Austria, Germany, France and Eastern Europe. Trains run to Genoa from Milan and from Nice.

Reservations for these services are essential You can book tickets for international journeys via **Eurail** and **Interrail**.
Eurail
w eurail.com
Interrail
w interrail.eu

Domestic Train Travel
Coastal Liguria has an excellent rail network, with frequent services, although they tend to be slower regional services, with a high-speed line between La Spezia and Genoa only (with no stops in between). Regionale (R) trains are the slower, stopping services; Regionale Veloce (RV) is a slightly faster service; Intercity trains are faster still, making only major stops. All these services are run by national rail operator **Trenitalia**; if you're heading out of Liguria to Milan, there are high-speed trains run by both Trenitalia and its private competitor, **Italo**. Always book tickets via the Trenitalia app.

In the Cinque Terre, Express trains run every 20 minutes between the five villages in summer. The best way to travel is by purchasing a Cinque Terre card (p178).
Italo Treno
w italotreno.it
Trenitalia
w trenitalia.com

GETTING TO AND FROM GENOVA CITY AIRPORT

Transport	Journey time	Fare
Bus (Volabus)	From 15 minutes	€6
Train + bus	7 minutes (transfer from Sestri Ponente station)	€1.50
Taxi	from 15 minutes	€25-30

JOURNEY PLANNER

Plotting Liguria's main train routes according to journey time, this map is a handy reference for train travel along the Riviera. Journey times are for the fastest available service.

••• **Direct train routes**

Genoa to La Spezia	1hr 4 min
Savona to Ventimiglia	1hr 20 min
Genoa to Savona	50 min
Camogli to Levanto	46 min
Riomaggiore to Monterosso	14 min
Imperia to Sanremo	15 min
La Spezia to Luni	19 min
Santa Margherita Ligure-Portofino to Rapallo	3 min
Albenga to Imperia	26 min
Genoa to Nervi	16 min

Long-Distance Coach Travel

Since most destinations on the Riviera are close to each other, it's easier to use the regional trains, but for longer distances, coach travel is a possibility, with Genoa the hub for destinations such as Savona and Sanremo. It's often cheaper by train, but coaches are an alternative to the packed rail network in the high season. Both **Flixbus** and **SITA** run coaches.

Flixbus
ⓦ flixbus.it
SITA
ⓦ sitabus.it

Public Transport

Genoa has an excellent public transport network run by **AMT Genova**, which controls the buses, metro, public lifts and funiculars in the city. It also has two main train stations – Genova Piazza Principe, in the lower part of town beside the Villa del Principe, and Genova Brignole. The latter is in the upper city, though it can be equidistant if not quicker to parts of the Centro Storico. Be aware that there's no public transport in the Centro Storico – the streets are too narrow. Even taxis may not be able to drop you to your exact destination.

Outside Genoa, public transport is more limited, though there are buses and trains for travellers without a car.

AMT
🔇 amt.genova.it

Tickets

Newspaper kiosks, tobacconists and bars sell tickets for public transport in Genoa – both singles (valid 100 minutes) and daily tickets. You can also buy 24-hour tickets online, and single tickets (valid 100 minutes) by text on Italian phones, by texting "AMT" to the number 850209.

Metro

Genoa's simple, one-line metro system covers most major tourist areas along its eight stations. More information on the city's metro map, as well as its history and prices can be found on the Mapa Metro website.

Mapa Metro
🔇 mapa-metro.com

Bus

There's an excellent bus network around Genoa, with hubs at Brignole, Piazza Principe, San Giorgio and Piazza de Ferrari. The latter two serve the top and bottom of the Centro Storico respectively.

The Cinque Terre has a number of electric buses running between the villages. Purchase a **Cinque Terre Card** online in advance for un-limited bus travel, as well as other advantages including access to local trains and the Sentiero Azzurro walking route.

Cinque Terre Card
🔇 card.parconazionale5terre.it/en

Taxis

There are taxi services all along the Riviera, although outside of the cities, prices may exceed what you'd expect – think upwards of €60 for the eight-mile journey from La Spezia to Riomaggiore. Taxis are not hailed; find one at an official stand (usually at the station or main piazza in towns), or reserve one by phone. In the smaller towns and villages, they tend to be one-person companies rather than the cooperatives of the cities – look out for business cards around town, or ask for recommendations. Ride-sharing apps such as Uber do not currently operate anywhere in Liguria.

Extra charges are added for each piece of luggage placed in the boot, for rides between 10pm and 7am, on Sundays and public holidays, and for journeys to and from airports.

Driving

Driving in Liguria can be a spectacular experience, with coast-hugging roads and beach towns to stop at every few miles. However, it can also be a significant challenge, with clogged roads in summer, winding mountain roads inland, and hair-raising, single-lane routes around iconic areas such as the Cinque Terre. Drivers with no experience of Ligurian roads may be surprised by the speed at which local drivers travel. Caution is always advised.

Parking is also a major issue, particularly on the Riviera di Levante, where most places of interest are small villages. Always book a local parking space through your accommodation if they offer it.

Driving to the Italian Riviera

If you are coming from within Italy, you'll likely arrive via the excellent *autostrada* (motorway) network. Crossing the nearby border from France is also easy, though there can be longer queues at the border in the summer months.

Driving in the Italian Riviera

If you bring your own foreign-registered car into Italy, you must carry a Green Card, the vehicle's registration documents, proof of car insurance, V5C registration certificate and a valid driver's licence. All non-EU-registered vehicles must also display a nationality sticker at the rear.

Towns and cities often enforce a Limited Traffic Zone (ZTL), which you must not drive into (unless prearranged with your accommodation). Tolls are payable on Liguria's *autostrade*, which run the length of the region, inland from the coast; payment is made at the end of the journey in cash or by credit card. Other roads don't incur tolls, and although the coastal roads can be clogged with traffic in summer, they're more scenic – Liguria's *autostrade* are essentially a series of tunnels cleaving through the mountains and cliffs.

Car Rental

To rent a car in Italy you must be over 21 and have held a valid driver's licence for at least a year. EU driving licences issued by any of the EU member states are valid throughout the European Union, including Italy. If visiting from outside the EU, you may need to apply for an International Driving Permit (IDP). Check with your local automobile association before you travel by car.

Rules of the Road

Drive on the right, use the left lane only for passing, and yield to traffic from the right. Seat belts are required for all passengers in the front and back, and heavy fines are levied for using a mobile phone while driving.

During the day, dipped headlights are compulsory when you are driving on the region's motorways, dual carriageways and on all out-of-town roads.

A red warning triangle, spare tyre and fluorescent vests must be carried at all times, for use in the event of an emergency.

If you have an accident or breakdown, switch on your hazard warning lights and place a warning triangle 50 m (164 ft) behind your vehicle. For breakdowns call the ACI emergency number (116) or the emergency services (112 or 113). The ACI will tow any foreign-registered car to the nearest ACI-affiliated garage for free.

Hitchhiking

Hitchhiking, or autostop, is illegal on motorways, and the narrowness of Liguria's rural roads makes it dangerous in many places. Always consider your own safety before entering an unknown vehicle.

Cycling

With sea views at every turn, cycling on the Riviera can be a joy, whether it's a short ride around the beachfront at Chiavari, or tackling the Riviera di Ponente's 24-km (15-mile) Pista Ciclabile (p170).

Mountain bikers will want to challenge themselves in the hinterland, too. The landscape around Finale Ligure attracts mountain bikers from around the world; **Atlas Ride Co** runs popular mountain biking holidays in the Riviera di Ponente.

In Genoa, cycling is a good option, though bicycles are prohibited in some of the busier sections of the Centro Storico.
Atlas Ride Co
Ⓦ atlasrideco.com

Bicycle Hire

Most resorts have bike hire companies – search for "noleggio bici" to find one near you, and ask them to advise on nearby trails and bike lanes. If you're on the Riviera di Levante, an e-bike is recommended due to the hilly terrain. In Genoa, companies like **Baja Bikes** and **Bike Fever** rent out a range of bicycles and e-bikes for all abilities. You may have to leave your passport

with the rental shop as a deposit, and you must have a valid licence to hire a bike.
Baja Bikes
Ⓦ bajabikes.eu
Bike Fever
Ⓦ bikefever.it

Bicycle Safety

Cycling is big in Italy, and drivers are by and large respectful of those on two wheels. Most of the seafront roads along the Riviera have relatively low speed limits, since they're in beachfront areas. That said, many Italians drive erratically, so only consider taking to the roads if you are a confident cyclist. Liguria's hilly terrain makes for some very steep ascents and descents.

Walking

Liguria has always been walking territory thanks to the mountainous landscape – and today, the region is crisscrossed with hiking trails, including the 600-km (370-mile) Sentiero Liguria, that follows the mountains for the length of the coast. The natural and national parks all have well-marked trails, and most hinterland areas have suggested hikes, too.

In the Cinque Terre, the Sentiero Azzurro links all of the five villages, though you will need a Cinque Terre Card to access the trails (p178). Note that the volume of foot traffic in the Cinque Terre has caused severe erosion of the cliffs in places, and sections of the route often close for maintenance. In Genoa, walking is the perfect way to see the city's architectural splendour, and many streets are pedestrianized, particularly in the Centro Storico.

Boats and Ferries

Ferries are a crucial mode of transport along much of the Riviera, with boats looping round the Portofino Peninsula, islands off Portovenere and the La Spezia-Levanto route along the Cinque Terre coastline. There are excursions to the latter from many resorts along the coast, too, as well as local trips from most resorts and villages to coves, diving areas and beautiful viewpoints. They're often a great alternative to the train when it comes to travel between overnight destinations – but always check you can take luggage onboard (there may also be a supplement to pay). There are plenty of routes leaving Genoa, if you want to arrive in style. Look at **Consorzio Marittimo Turistico Cinque Terre** or **Servizio Marittimo del Tigullio** for local schedules and fares.
Consorzio Marittimo Turistico Cinque Terre
Ⓦ navigazionegolfodeipoeti.it
Servizio Marittimo del Tigullio
Ⓦ traghettiportofino.it

PRACTICAL
INFORMATION

Forward planning is essential for any successful trip. Prepare yourself for any eventuality by brushing up on the following points before you set off.

AT A GLANCE

EMERGENCY NUMBERS

GENERAL EMERGENCY

113

AMBULANCE

118

FIRE SERVICE

115

POLICE

112

TIME ZONE
CET/CEST Central European Summer Time runs from the last Sunday in March to the last Sunday in October.

TAP WATER
Unless stated otherwise, tap water is safe to drink.

WEBSITES AND APPS

Pronto Treno
A useful app for buying train tickets as well as checking times.

La Mia Liguria
Liguria's official tourism website (www.lamialiguria.it) contains a host of seasonal itineraries and information on the region.

Genova More Than This
Genoa's official tourism website (www.visitgenoa.it) provides useful up-to-date information on events.

Personal Security

Italy is a relatively safe place to visit, and Liguria even more so, but you should still take precautions to avoid incidents. Pickpockets can be a problem in cities and crowded tourist sites such as Portofino and Cinque Terre – particularly when getting on and off trains. Always keep your belongings within eyesight during train journeys and at stations.

Italians are relatively accepting of all people, regardless of their race, gender or sexuality. Homosexuality was legalized in Italy in 1887, and in 1982, Italy became the third country to recognize the right to legally change your gender. Genoa in particular is extremely cosmopolitan – one of Italy's true multiracial cities, it's also LGBTQ+-friendly and has a thriving red light district in the Centro Storico. Away from the city and the bustling coastal resorts, life inland is far more traditional and conservative, though outright hostility is rare. If you do feel unsafe, the **Safe Space Alliance** pinpoints your nearest place of refuge.

Women may receive unwanted and unwelcome attention, particularly in the form of unsolicited compliments or jeers, especially around tourist areas. If you feel threatened, head straight for the nearest police station.
Safe Space Alliance
🅦 safespacealliance.com

Health

Italy has a world-class healthcare system. Emergency medical care in Italy is free for all EU and Australian citizens. If you have an EHIC or GHIC (p175), be sure to present this as soon as possible. You may have to pay after treatment and reclaim the money later. For visitors from outside the EU and Australia, payment of medical expenses is the patient's responsibility. As such, it is important to arrange comprehensive medical insurance.

Seek medicinal supplies and advice for minor ailments from a pharmacy (farmacia). You can find details of the nearest 24-hour service on all pharmacy doors. Be aware that although most

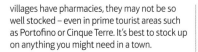

villages have pharmacies, they may not be so well stocked – even in prime tourist areas such as Portofino or Cinque Terre. It's best to stock up on anything you might need in a town.

Smoking, Alcohol and Drugs

Smoking and vaping are banned in all public spaces. However, many bars and restaurants have outdoor areas where smoking is permitted. The possession of illegal drugs is prohibited and could result in a prison sentence.

Italy has a strict limit of 0.05 per cent BAC (blood alcohol content) for drivers. This means that you cannot drink more than a small beer or a small glass of wine if you plan to drive. For drivers with less than three years' driving experience, and those under 21, the limit is 0.

ID

By law you must carry identification at all times in Italy. A photocopy of your passport photo page (and visa if applicable) should suffice. If you are stopped by the police you may be asked to present the original document within 12 hours of the initial request.

Local Customs

Italians are relatively relaxed when it comes to etiquette. Strangers usually shake hands, while friends and family greet each other with a kiss on each cheek. But there are some strict rules. In Genoa you can be fined for dropping litter, sitting on monument steps, or eating or drinking outside churches and monuments. It is an offence to bathe in public fountains.

Visiting Churches and Cathedrals

Entrance to churches is free, but you may be charged a small fee to see a certain area, such as a chapel, cloister or underground ruins. Visiting may be prohibited during Mass. Strict dress codes usually apply but are not always enforced: cover your torso and upper arms, and ensure shorts and skirts cover your knees. Shoes must be worn. In some places of worship photography is banned. Many of the region's churches keep sporadic opening hours.

Responsible Travel

Overtourism has a major impact on Liguria – particularly in the Riviera di Levante, where the Cinque Terre and Portofino have serious problems with visitor numbers. Numerous measures have been implemented to prevent overcrowding: fines can be levied to tourists stopping in Portofino's busy areas, and booking systems have been applied to some of the region's walking trails. When visiting, try not to stop to take photos in congested areas, and take public transport to reduce traffic on the roads. It's also advised that you head beyond the popular villages and make for the quieter vineyards, clifftop trails and lesser-known hamlets. Visiting out of the summer season is an excellent way of avoiding crowds.

The climate crisis is also threatening the Riviera, with heavy rain causing severe damage, particularly in cliffside locations. The Cinque Terre's fragile landscape is in real danger from climate change, as highlighted by the severe flooding in 2011. When walking in the region, ensure you stick to designated trails to prevent erosion of the cliffs.

Mobile Phones and Wi-Fi

Wi-Fi is generally widely available throughout Italy, and cafés and restaurants will often permit the use of their Wi-Fi on the condition that you make a purchase.

Post

Post offices are prominently located in Genoa and in town squares. Stamps can be bought from both post offices and newspaper kiosks.

Note that letters and postcards can take a long time to arrive at their destinations.

Taxes and Refunds

VAT (called IVA in Italy) is usually 22 per cent, with a reduced rate of 4 to 10 per cent on some items. Non-EU citizens can claim an IVA rebate subject to certain conditions. It is easier to claim before you buy. If claiming retrospectively, at the airport, present a customs officer with your purchases and a *fattura* receipt, with your name and the amount of IVA on the item purchased.

INDEX

Page numbers in **bold** refer to main entries.

PHRASE BOOK

IN EMERGENCY

Help!	Aiuto!	eye-**yoo**-toh
Stop!	Fermate!	fair-**mah**-teh
Call a doctor.	Chiama un medico.	kee-**ah**-mah oon **meh**-dee-koh
Call an ambulance.	Chiama un' ambulanza.	kee-**ah**-mah oon am-boo-lan-tsa
Call the police.	Chiama la polizia.	kee-**ah**-mah lah pol-ee-**tsee**-ah
Call the fire brigade.	Chiama i pompieri.	kee-**ah**-mah ee pom-pee-**air**-ee
Where is the telephone?	Dov'è il telefono?	dov-**eh** eel teh-**leh**-foh-noh?
The nearest hospital?	L'ospedale più vicino?	loss-peh-**dah**-leh pee-**oo** vee-**chee**-noh?

COMMUNICATION ESSENTIALS

Yes/No	Sì/No	see/noh
Please	Per favore	pair fah-**vor**-eh
Thank you	Grazie	grah-tsee-eh
Excuse me	Mi scusi	mee **skoo**-zee
Hello	Buon giorno	bwon jor-noh
Goodbye	Arrivederci	ah-ree-veh-dair-chee
Good evening	Buona sera	bwon-ah **sair**-ah
morning	la mattina	lah mah-**tee**-nah
afternoon	il pomeriggio	eel poh-meh-**ree**-joh
evening	la sera	lah **sair**-ah
yesterday	ieri	ee-**air**-ee
today	oggi	oh-jee
tomorrow	domani	doh-**mah**-nee
here	qui	kwee
there	la	lah
What?	Quale?	**kwah**-leh?
When?	Quando?	**kwan**-doh?
Why?	Perchè?	pair-**keh**?
Where?	Dove?	**doh**-veh?

USEFUL PHRASES

How are you?	Come sta?	koh-meh stah?
Very well, thank you.	Molto bene, grazie.	moll-toh **beh**-neh grah-tsee-eh
Pleased to meet you.	Piacere di conoscerla.	pee-ah-**chair**-eh dee coh-**noh**-shair-lah
See you later.	A più tardi.	ah pee-**oo** tar-dee
That's fine.	Va bene.	va **beh**-neh
Where is/are ...?	Dov'è/Dove sono ...?	dov-**eh**/doveh soh-noh?
How long does it take to get to ...?	Quanto tempo ci vuole per andare a ...?	kwan-toh tem-poh chee voo-**oh**-leh pair an-dar-eh ah ...?
How do I get to ...?	Come faccio per arrivare a ...?	koh-meh fah-choh pair arri-var-eh ah ...?
Do you speak English?	Parla inglese?	par-lah een-gleh-zeh?
I don't understand.	Non capisco.	non ka-pee-skoh
Could you speak more slowly, please?	Può parlare più lentamente, per favore?	pwoh par-lah-reh pee-**oo** len-ta-men-teh pair fah-**vor**-eh?
I'm sorry.	Mi dispiace.	mee dee-spee-ah-cheh

USEFUL WORDS

big	grande	gran-deh
small	piccolo	**pee**-koh-loh
hot	caldo	kal-doh
cold	freddo	fred-doh
good	buono	bwoh-noh
bad	cattivo	kat-**tee**-voh
enough	basta	bas-tah
well	bene	**beh**-neh
open	aperto	ah-**pair**-toh
closed	chiuso	kee-**oo**-zoh
left	a sinistra	ah see-nee-strah
right	a destra	ah dess-trah
straight on	sempre dritto	sem-preh dree-toh
near	vicino	vee-**chee**-noh
far	lontano	lon-**tah**-noh
up	su	soo
down	giù	joo
early	presto	press-toh
late	tardi	tar-dee
entrance	entrata	en-**trah**-tah
exit	uscita	oo-**shee**-ta
toilet	il gabinetto	eel gah-bee-**net**-toh
free, unoccupied	libero	lee-**bair**-oh
free, no charge	gratuito	grah-**too**-ee-toh

MAKING A TELEPHONE CALL

I'd like to place a long-distance call.	Vorrei fare una interurbana.	vor-**ray** far-eh oona in-tair-oor-**bah**-nah
I'd like to make a reverse-charge call.	Vorrei fare una telefonata a carico del destinatario.	vor-**ray** far-eh oona teh-leh-fon-ah-tah ah kar-ee-koh dell dess-tee-nah-tar-ee-oh
I'll try again later.	Ritelefono più tardi.	ree-teh-**leh**-foh-noh pee-oo tar-dee
Can I leave a message?	Posso lasciare un messaggio?	**poss**-oh lash-ah-reh oon mess-**sah**-joh?
Hold on.	Un attimo, per favore	oon ah-tee-moh, pair fah-**vor**-eh
Could you speak up a little please?	Può parlare più forte, per favore?	pwoh par-**lah**-reh pee-oo for-teh, pair fah-**vor**-eh?
local call	telefonata locale	te-leh-fon-**ah**-tah loh-cah-leh

SHOPPING

How much does this cost?	Quant'è, per favore?	kwan-**teh** pair fah-vor-eh?
I would like ...	Vorrei ...	vor-**ray**
Do you have ...?	Avete ...?	ah-veh-teh...?
I'm just looking.	Sto soltanto guardando.	stoh sol-**tan**-toh gwar-**dan**-doh
Do you take credit cards?	Accettate carte di credito?	ah-chet-tah-teh kar-teh dee creh-dee-toh?
What time do you open/close?	A che ora apre/ chiude?	ah keh or-ah ah-preh/kee-oo-deh?
this one	questo	kweh-stoh
that one	quello	kwell-oh
expensive	caro	kar-oh
cheap	a buon prezzo	ah bwon pret-soh
size, clothes	la taglia	lah tah-lee-ah
size, shoes	il numero	eel **noo**-mair-oh
white	bianco	bee-ang-koh
black	nero	neh-roh
red	rosso	ross-oh
yellow	giallo	jal-loh
green	verde	vair-deh
blue	blu	bloo

TYPES OF SHOP

antique dealer	l'antiquario	lan-tee-**kwah**-ree-oh
bakery	il forno /il panificio	eel **forn**-oh /eel pan-ee-**fee**-choh
bank	la banca	lah bang-kah
bookshop	la libreria	lah lee-breh-**ree**-ah
butcher	la macelleria	lah mah-chell-eh-**ree**-ah
cake shop	la pasticceria	lah pas-tee-chair-**ee**-ah
chemist	la farmacia	lah far-mah-**chee**-ah
delicatessen	la salumeria	lah sah-loo-meh-**ree**-ah
department store	il grande magazzino	eel **gran**-deh mag-gad-**zee**-noh
fishmonger	il pescivendolo	eel pesh-ee-**ven**-doh-loh
florist	il fioraio	eel fee-or-**eye**-oh
greengrocer	il fruttivendolo	eelfroo-tee-ven-doh-loh
grocery	alimentari	ah-lee-men-**tah**-ree
hairdresser	il parrucchiere	eel par-oo-kee-**air**-eh
ice cream parlour	la gelateria	lah jel-lah-tair-**ree**-ah
market	il mercato	eel mair-**kah**-toh
newsstand	l'edicola	leh-**dee**-koh-lah
post office	l'ufficio postale	loo-**fee**-choh pos-**tah**-leh
shoe shop	il negozio di scarpe	eel neh-**goh**-tsioh dee **skar**-peh
supermarket	il supermercato	eelsu-pair-mair-**kah**-toh
tobacconist	il tabaccaio	eel tah-bak-**eye**-oh
travel agency	l'agenzia di viaggi	lah-jen-**tsee**-ah dee vee-**ad**-jee

SIGHTSEEING

art gallery	la pinacoteca	lahpeena-koh-**teh**-kah
bus stop	la fermata dell'autobus	lah fair-**mah**-tah dell ow-toh-booss
church	la chiesa	lah kee-eh-zah
	la basilica	lah bah-**seel**-i-kah
closed for holidays	chiuso per le ferie	kee-oo-zoh pair leh **fair**-ee-eh
garden	il giardino	eel jar-**dee**-no
library	la biblioteca	lah beeb-lee-oh-**teh**-kah
museum	il museo	eel moo-**zeh**-oh
railway station	la stazione	lah stah-tsee-oh-neh
tourist information	l'ufficio di turismo	loo-**fee**-choh dee too-**ree**-smoh

STAYING IN A HOTEL

Do you have any vacant rooms?	**Avete camere libere?**	*ah-veh-teh kah-mair-eh lee-bair-eh?*
double room	**una camera doppia**	*oona kah-mair-ah doh-pee-ah*
with double bed	**con letto matrimoniale**	*kon let-toh mah-tree-moh-nee-ah-leh*
twin room	**una camera con due letti**	*oona kah-mair-ah kon doo-eh let-tee*
single room	**una camera singola**	*oona kah-mair-ah sing-goh-lah*
room with a bath, shower	**una camera con bagno, con doccia**	*oona kah-mair-ah kon ban-yoh, kon dot-chah*
porter	**il facchino**	*eel fah-kee-noh*
key	**la chiave**	*lah kee-ah-veh*
I have a reservation.	**Ho fatto una prenotazione.**	*oh fat-toh oona preh-noh-tah-tsee-oh-neh*

EATING OUT

Have you got a table for ...?	**Avete una tavola per ... ?**	*ah-veh-teh oona tah-voh-lah pair ...?*
I'd like to reserve a table.	**Vorrei riservare una tavola.**	*vor-ray ree-sair-vah-reh oona tah-voh-lah*
breakfast	**colazione**	*koh-lah-tsee-oh-neh*
lunch	**pranzo**	*pran-tsoh*
dinner	**cena**	*cheh-nah*
The bill, please.	**Il conto, per favore.**	*eel kon-toh pair fah-vor-eh*
I am a vegetarian.	**Sono vegetariano/a.**	*soh-noh veh-jeh-tar-ee-ah-noh/nah*
waitress	**cameriera**	*kah-mair-ee-air-ah*
waiter	**cameriere**	*kah-mair-ee-air-eh*
fixed price menu	**il menù a prezzo fisso**	*eel meh-noo ah pret-soh fee-soh*
dish of the day	**piatto del giorno**	*pee-ah-toh del jor-no*
starter	**antipasto**	*an-tee-pass-toh*
first course	**il primo**	*eel pree-moh*
main course	**il secondo**	*eel seh-kon-doh*
vegetables	**il contorno**	*eel kon-tor-noh*
dessert	**il dolce**	*eel doll-cheh*
cover charge	**il coperto**	*eel koh-pair-toh*
wine list	**la lista dei vini**	*lah lee-stah day vee-nee*
rare	**al sangue**	*al sang-gweh*
medium	**al puntino**	*al poon-tee-noh*
well done	**ben cotto**	*ben kot-toh*
glass	**il bicchiere**	*eel bee-kee-air-eh*
bottle	**la bottiglia**	*lah bot-teel-yah*
knife	**il coltello**	*eel kol-tell-oh*
fork	**la forchetta**	*lah for-ket-tah*
spoon	**il cucchiaio**	*eel koo-kee-eye-oh*

MENU DECODER

l'acqua minerale gassata/naturale	*lah-kwah mee-nair-ah-leh gah-zah-tah/ nah-too-rah-leh*	mineral water fizzy/still
agnello	*ah-niell-oh*	lamb
aceto	*ah-cheh-toh*	vinegar
aglio	*al-ee-oh*	garlic
al forno	*al for-noh*	baked
alla griglia	*ah-lah greel-yah*	grilled
l'aragosta	*lah-rah-goss-tah*	lobster
arrosto	*ar-ross-toh*	roast
la birra	*lah beer-rah*	beer
la bistecca	*lah bee-stek-kah*	steak
il brodo	*eel broh-doh*	broth
il burro	*eel boor-oh*	butter
il caffè	*eel kah-feh*	coffee
i calamari	*ee kah-lah-mah-ree*	squid
i carciofi	*ee kar-choff-ee*	artichokes
la carne	*la kar-neh*	meat
carne di maiale	*kar-neh dee mah-yah-leh*	pork
la cipolla	*la chip-oh-lah*	onion
i contorni	*ee kon-tor-nee*	vegetables
i fagioli	*ee fah-joh-lee*	beans
il fegato	*eel fay-gah-toh*	liver
il finocchio	*eel fee-nok-ee-oh*	fennel
il formaggio	*eel for-mad-joh*	cheese
le fragole	*leh frah-goh-leh*	strawberries
il fritto misto	*eel free-toh mees-toh*	mixed fried dish
la frutta	*la froot-tah*	fruit
frutti di mare	*froo-tee dee mah-reh*	seafood
i funghi	*ee foon-ghee*	mushrooms
i gamberi	*ee gam-bair-ee*	prawns
il gelato	*eel jel-lah-toh*	ice cream
l'insalata	*leen-sah-lah-tah*	salad
il latte	*eel laht-teh*	milk
lesso	*less-oh*	boiled
il manzo	*eel man-tsoh*	beef
la melanzana	*lah meh-lan-tsah-nah*	aubergine
la minestra	*lah mee-ness-trah*	soup
l'olio	*loh-lee-oh*	oil
il pane	*eel pah-neh*	bread
le patate	*leh pah-tah-teh*	potatoes
le patatine fritte	*leh pah-tah-teen-eh free-teh*	chips
il pepe	*eel peh-peh*	pepper
la pesca	*lah pess-kah*	peach
il pesce	*eel pesh-eh*	fish
il pollo	*eel poll-oh*	chicken
il pomodoro	*eel poh-moh-dor-oh*	tomato
il prosciutto cotto/crudo	*eel pro-shoo-toh kot-toh/kroo-doh*	ham cooked/cured
il riso	*eel ree-zoh*	rice
il sale	*eel sah-leh*	salt
la salsiccia	*lah sal-see-chah*	sausage
le seppie	*leh sep-pee-eh*	cuttlefish
secco	*sek-koh*	dry
la sogliola	*lah soll-yoh-lah*	sole
i spinaci	*ee spee-nah-chee*	spinach
succo d'arancia/ di limone	*soo-koh dah-ran-chah/ dee lee-moh-neh*	orange/lemon juice
il tè	*eel teh*	tea
la tisana	*lah tee-zah-nah*	herbal tea
il tonno	*eel ton-noh*	tuna
la torta	*lah tor-tah*	cake/tart
l'uovo	*loo-oh-voh*	egg
vino bianco	*vee-noh bee-ang-koh*	white wine
vino rosso	*vee-noh ross-oh*	red wine
il vitello	*eel vee-tell-oh*	veal
le vongole	*leh von-goh-leh*	clams
lo zucchero	*loh zoo-kair-oh*	sugar
gli zucchini	*lyee dzu-kee-nee*	courgettes
la zuppa	*lah tsoo-pah*	soup

NUMBERS

1	**uno**	*oo-noh*
2	**due**	*doo-eh*
3	**tre**	*treh*
4	**quattro**	*kwat-roh*
5	**cinque**	*ching-kweh*
6	**sei**	*say-ee*
7	**sette**	*set-teh*
8	**otto**	*ot-toh*
9	**nove**	*noh-veh*
10	**dieci**	*dee-eh-chee*
11	**undici**	*oon-dee-chee*
12	**dodici**	*doh-dee-chee*
13	**tredici**	*tray-dee-chee*
14	**quattordici**	*kwat-tor-dee-chee*
15	**quindici**	*kwin-dee-chee*
16	**sedici**	*say-dee-chee*
17	**diciassette**	*dee-chah-set-teh*
18	**diciotto**	*dee-chot-toh*
19	**diciannove**	*dee-chah-noh-veh*
20	**venti**	*ven-tee*
30	**trenta**	*tren-tah*
40	**quaranta**	*kwah-ran-tah*
50	**cinquanta**	*ching-kwan-tah*
60	**sessanta**	*sess-an-tah*
70	**settanta**	*set-tan-tah*
80	**ottanta**	*ot-tan-tah*
90	**novanta**	*noh-van-tah*
100	**cento**	*chen-toh*
1,000	**mille**	*mee-leh*
2,000	**duemila**	*doo-eh mee-lah*
5,000	**cinquemila**	*ching-kweh mee-lah*
1,000,000	**un milione**	*oon meel-yoh-neh*

TIME

one minute	**un minuto**	*oon mee-noo-toh*
one hour	**un'ora**	*oon or-ah*
half an hour	**mezz'ora**	*medz-or-ah*
a day	**un giorno**	*oon jor-noh*
a week	**una settimana**	*oona set-tee-mah-nah*
Monday	**lunedì**	*loo-neh-dee*
Tuesday	**martedì**	*mar-teh-dee*
Wednesday	**mercoledì**	*mair-koh-leh-dee*
Thursday	**giovedì**	*joh-veh-dee*
Friday	**venerdì**	*ven-air-dee*
Saturday	**sabato**	*sah-bah-toh*
Sunday	**domenica**	*doh-meh-nee-kah*

ACKNOWLEDGMENTS

DK would like to thank the following for their contribution to the previous editions: Fabrizio Ardito, Sonia Cavicchioli, Maurizia De Martin, Gianluigi Lanza, Julia Buckley, Kiki Deere, Toni de Bella

The publisher would like to thank the following for their kind permission to reproduce their photographs:

(Key: a-above; b-below/bottom; c-centre; f-far; l-left; r-right; t-top)

123RF.com: Boryana Yordanova Manzurova 70-71t

4Corners: Davide Erbetta 160bl

Alamy Stock Photo: AGB Photo Library 88-89t, AGF Srl / Hermes Images 22-23t, Album 81ca, Art Collection 4 81crb, Suzy Bennett 116bl, Stephen Bisgrove 42clb, Richard Broadwell 49cra, Michael Brooks 16c, 50-51, 75tl, Sunny Celeste 132br, Chronicle 45crb, ClickAlps Srls 37br, ClickAlps Srls / Marco Bottigelli 20tl, Colaimages 48cb, Roberto Contini 11t, Ian Dagnall 90-91t, Wendy Kaveney / Jaynes Gallery / Danita Delimont, Agent 43cla, Svetlana Day 4, Pavel Dudek 11cr, escapetheofficejob 120-121b, Andrew Fare 44t, Manfred Gottschalk 74bl, GRANGER - Historical Picture Archive 44cb, Andrew Hasson 22cla, Gardel Bertrand / Hemis.fr 18crb, 88bl, Mattes Ren / Hemis.fr 10clb, 29ca, 31tr, 35br, 71br, 115t, Moirenc Camille / Hemis.fr 25cla, Rieger Bertrand / Hemis.fr 23tr, 157t, James Hodgson 150bl, 151tl, Peter Horree 47cra, Image Professionals GmbH / Daniel Schoenen 12-13b, 168t, Image Professionals GmbH / LOOK-foto 172-173, Imagebroker / Arco / F. Schneider 80-81b, imageBROKER / Guenter Graefenhain 86-87bc, imageBROKER.com GmbH & Co. KG / Daniel Schoenen 41cla, 168cra, incamerastock / ICP 45bl, Japhotos 18cr, 98cra, Jon Arnold Images Ltd 24-25t, Brenda Kean 101br, mauritius images GmbH / ClickAlps 24-25b, 171br, NurPhoto SRL 49tr, Old Books Images 44bl, 89br, Old Images 47tr, Panther Media GmbH / Fabio Lotti / faabi 22tl, parkerphotography 30-31b, 154bl, Photo12 / Coll-DITE / USIS 48tl, Anna Pozzi 109cb, Prisma Archivo 46tl, Really Easy Star 46br, Really Easy Star / Toni Spagone 21tr, 25crb, 32tl, 68b, 72-73b, 81cra, 81br, 82t, 124-125t, 125tc, RealyEasyStar / Claudio Pagliarani 139bl, REDA &CO srl 152, 162tl, 169br, REDA &CO srl / Eddy Buttarelli 159tr, Reda and Co 55t, 76-77, robertharding / Gavin Hellier 49bl, robertharding / ProCip 8cl, Alexandre Rotenberg 129tr, Christoph Rueegg 126br, Riccardo Sala 149tc, 151br, Peter Sampson 43cra, SFL Travel 41br, Michal Sikorski 60bl, 140bl, 146-147t, snabsa 166-167t, Geoffrey Taunton 67br, The Granger Collection 47bl, travelbild-Italy 144b, 166bl, Universal Images Group North America LLC / marka / nevio doz 42cl, Ivan Vdovin 161tr, wanderluster 28br, Washington Imaging 148t, Jrgen Weginger 28-29t, Jan Wlodarczyk 26-27t, World History Archive 46-47t

AWL Images: Marco Bottigelli 122-123t, ClickAlps 10-11b, 128b, 154-155t, Marco Simoni 108-109b, Catherina Unger 2-3, 12clb, 55bl, 92

Bridgeman Images: © A. De Gregorio / © NPL - DeA Picture Library 47cb, © British Library Board. All Rights Reserved 46cb, © Look and Learn 45tl, 48bc, Photo © Claudio Beduschi / Cuboimages 48-49t

Depositphotos Inc: Garsya 124bl, scrisman 163cra

Dreamstime.com: Andmorg 8cla, Davide Angelini 30tr, Arkantostock 127t, Bapaume 20cla, 98t, Valerio Bianchi 49crb, Arkadi Bojarinov 37cr, Julia Burlachenko 142-143t, Byvalet 141tr, Valeria Cantone 42cr, Ioan Florin Cnejevici 62-63t, Coffeechocolates 13br, Crackerclips 114b, Svetlana Day 13cr, 31cla, Dudlajzov 18bl, 39tr, Sergey Dzyuba 164b, Domenico Farone 17bl, 134-135, Kirk Fisher 26bl, 102-103, Frantic00 10ca, Apostolos Giontzis 32-33b, Janoka82 132t, Oleksandr Korzhenko 12t, Iuliia Lavrinenko 36-37t, Lianem 11br, Luca Lorenzelli 110-111b, Fabio Lotti 84bl, 110tr, 146bl, Lucagal 40-41t, Alberto Masnovo 27br, Maudanros 156bl, Krisztian Miklosy 20-21ca, Sean Pavone 18t, 100-101t, 118-119t, Andriy Petrenko 71tc, David Pillow 72cra, Fabrizio Robba 34-35t, 43tr, 43crb, 69tl, 84-85t, Davide Romanini 96-97b, Stevanzz 133br, Travnikovstudio 17t, 104-105, Xantana 171tl, Zoom-zoom 54c, 56-57

Getty Images: AFP / Tiziana Fabi / Stringer 42cla, Fabio Bussalino 42crb, De Agostini Picture Library 45tr, DEA / A. Dagli Orti 45cra, Alessandro Levati 13t, Jacopo M. Raule / Stringer 42cra, Universal Images Group / Marka 48cr, Universal Images Group / REDA&CO 158b, Vittorio Sciosia / REDA&CO / Universal Images Group 33cla, Velo / Tim de Waele / Staff 43tl, Westend61 117tr

Getty Images / iStock: Matteo Bertetto 39cl, bluejayphoto 6-7, E+ / Imgorthand 40bl, Orietta Gaspari 66t, MicheleVacchiano 43clb, PK-Photos 8clb, StevanZZ 112-113t

Shutterstock.com: arkanto 36bl, Valeria Cantone 157cra, Marti Bug Catcher 130-131t, D-VISIONS 119bl, faber1893 38-39b, 94-95t, 99br, Stefano Fei 131cra, LifeCollectionPhotography 27cr, lucamarimedia 138-139t, MarkUK97 35ca, maudanros 29br, Mathias Pabst 34bl, Zharov Pavel 20-21t, Stefano Peracchia 163b, Antonio Petrone 38tr, Andrea Raffin 33tr, Valenti Renzo 158clb, S1001 64bl, Simona Sirio 22-23ca, 165tl, Stella Photography 60clb, trabantos 80tr, King Tut 60bc, ValerioMei 64-65t, 86tl, Olena Znak 8-9

Cover images: *Front and Spine:* **AWL Images:** Matteo Colombo; *Back:* **Alamy Stock Photo:** imageBROKER / Guenter Graefenhain cla; **AWL Images:** Matteo Colombo b; **Dreamstime.com:** Lianem t, Fabio Lotti c; *Front Flap:* **Alamy Stock Photo:** Ian Dagnall cra, Rieger Bertrand / Hemis.fr cb, REDA &CO srl bl, Michal Sikorski cla; **Depositphotos Inc:** Garsya t; **Shutterstock.com:** King Tut br

All other images © Dorling Kindersley

Illustrators: Andrea Barison, Gianluca Fiorani

Contributors Fabrizio Ardito, Sonia Cavicchioli, Maurizia De Martin, Gianluigi Lanza, Julia Buckley, Kiki Deere, Toni de Bella
Senior Editors Zoë Rutland, Dipika Dasgupta
Senior Designer Stuti Tiwari
Project Editors Alex Pathe, Anuroop Sanwalia
Project Art Editor Bharti Karakoti
Editors Anjasi N.N, Nandini Desiraju
Proofreader Stephanie Smith
Indexer Helen Peters
Picture Research Manpreet Kaur, Nishwan Rasool
Publishing Assistant Simona Velikova
Jacket Designer Bharti Karakoti, Laura O'Brien
Cartography Manager Suresh Kumar
Senior Cartographic Editor Subhashree Bharati
Senior DTP Designer Tanveer Zaidi
Senior Production Editor Jason Little
Production Controller Kariss Ainsworth
Managing Editors Shikha Kulkarni, Beverley Smart, Hollie Teague
Managing Art Editor Priyanka Thakur
Art Director Maxine Pedliham
Publishing Director Georgina Dee

First edition 2005

Published in Great Britain by Dorling Kindersley Limited,
DK, One Embassy Gardens, 8 Viaduct Gardens,
London SW11 7BW, UK

The authorised representative in the EEA is
Dorling Kindersley Verlag GmbH. Arnulfstr.
124, 80636 Munich, Germany

Published in the United States by DK Publishing,
1745 Broadway, 20th Floor, New York, NY 10019, USA

Copyright © 2005, 2024 Dorling Kindersley Limited
A Penguin Random House Company

24 25 26 27 10 9 8 7 6 5 4 3 2 1

The publishers cannot accept responsibility for any consequences
arising from the use of this book, nor for any material on third
party websites, and cannot guarantee that any website address in
this book will be a suitable source of travel information.

A CIP catalog record for this book
is available from the British Library.

A catalog record for this book is available
from the Library of Congress.

ISSN: 1542 1554
ISBN: 978 0 2414 7084 8

Printed and bound in China.

www.dk.com

A NOTE FROM DK EYEWITNESS

The rate at which the world is changing is constantly
keeping the DK Eyewitness team on our toes. While
we've worked hard to ensure that this edition of Italian
Riviera is accurate and up-to-date, we know that
opening hours alter, standards shift, prices fluctuate,
places close and new ones pop up in their stead. So, if
you notice we've got something wrong or left something
out, we want to hear about it. Please get in touch at
travelguides@dk.com